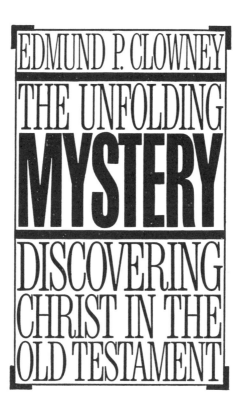

EDMUND P. CLOWNEY
THE UNFOLDING MYSTERY
DISCOVERING CHRIST IN THE OLD TESTAMENT

D0822746

P.O.BOX 817 • PHILLIPSBURG • NEW JERSEY 08865

ISBN-10: 0-87552-174-6
ISBN-13: 978-0-87552-174-9

Printed in the United States of America

CONTENTS

THE AUTHOR

Edmund P. Clowney taught practical theology at Westminster Theological Seminary from 1952 to 1984 and served as president of the seminary from 1966 to 1982. He received a Th.B. from Westminster, an S.T.M. from Yale Divinity School, and a D.D. from Wheaton College.

A visionary educator and church leader, Dr. Clowney is perhaps best remembered as the leading proponent and practitioner of redemptive-historical preaching in recent decades. His books include *Preaching and Biblical Theology*, *Called to the Ministry*, *Doctrine of the Church*, and *The Message of 1 Peter*.

FOREWORD

The Bible is a unity. That is, perhaps, the most amazing of all the amazing things that are true of it. It consists of sixty-six separate units, written over more than a thousand years against a wide variety of cultural backgrounds, by people who for the most part worked independently of each other and show no awareness that their books would become canonical Scripture. The books themselves are of all kinds: prose jostling poetry, hymns rubbing shoulders with history, sermons with statistics, letters with liturgies, lurid visions with a love song.

Why do we bind up this collection between the same two covers, call it *The Holy Bible*, and treat it as one book? One justification for doing this—one of many—is that the collection as a whole, once we start to explore it, proves to have an organic coherence that is simply stunning. Books written centuries apart seem to have been designed for the express purpose of supplementing and illuminating each other. There is throughout one leading character (God the Creator), one historical perspective (world redemption), one focal figure (Jesus of Nazareth, who is both Son of God and Savior), and one solid body of harmonious teaching about God and godliness. Truly the inner unity of the Bible is miraculous: a sign and a wonder, challenging the unbelief of our skeptical age.

Biblical theology is the umbrella-name for those disciplines that explore the unity of the Bible, delving into the contents of the books, showing the links between them, and pointing up the ongoing flow of the revelatory and redemptive process that reached its climax in Jesus Christ. Historical exegesis, which explores what the text meant and implied for its original readership, is one of these disciplines. Typology, which looks into Old Testament patterns of divine action, agency, and instruction that found final fulfillment in Christ, is another.

In both these arts, Edmund Clowney is a veteran and a master, combining in himself the sobriety of a wise and learned head with the exuberance of a warm and worshiping heart. *The Unfolding Mystery*, a study of the Old Testament frame for understanding Jesus, is vintage Clowney.

The importance of this theme—the Old Testament pointing to Christ—is great, although for half a century Bible teachers, possibly embarrassed by the memory of too-fanciful ventures into typology in the past, have not made much of it. (Its abiding importance, we might say, is commensurate with its current neglect!) For this reason, Dr. Clowney's admirable treatment of it should be greatly valued; it fills a gap, and supplies a felt need.

Expect your heart to be stirred, as well as your head cleared, as you read.

DR. J. I. PACKER

INTRODUCTION

"The Greatest Story Ever Told"—this title has been used for the Bible, and with good reason. The Bible is the greatest storybook, not just because it is full of wonderful stories but because it tells one *great* story, the story of Jesus. That story is still being told to thousands who hear it for the first time—perhaps in a Hong Kong apartment, or in an American university dormitory.

But where in the Bible does the old, old story begin? Not in the manger of a Bethlehem stable, but earlier. How much earlier? Luke's Gospel begins the story at least a full year before the birth of Jesus.

An old priest, Zechariah, was standing by the altar of incense in the Temple at Jerusalem. Suddenly he was not alone in the sanctuary. An angel stood there beside him: "Do not be afraid, Zechariah; your prayer has been heard" (Lk. 1:13). The angel then announced to Zechariah that he would have a son, John. The marvel was not simply that an elderly childless couple would have a son, but that their son would be a prophet. Centuries had passed since God last spoke through the prophets. But God would make John like the ancient prophet Elijah. John would be the forerunner of the coming Lord.

Clearly the announcement of the angel to Zechariah was not the beginning for Luke, even though he took up the story there. The birth of John fulfilled an old prophecy: "See, I will send you the prophet Elijah before that great and dreadful day of the LORD comes" (Mal. 4:5). That prophecy is found on the last page of the Old Testament. But that was not the beginning either.

To discover the start of the story, we must go back to read about Elijah and find out how he prepared for the coming of the Lord. How far back must we go in order to begin at the very beginning? Luke gives us a dramatic answer when he provides the legal genealogy of Jesus (Lk. 3:23-37). The royal line goes back through Zerubbabel, Nathan, David, to the tribe of Judah, then to Abraham, then to Shem, Noah, and Seth, "the son of Adam, the son of God."

Luke would have us understand that the story of Jesus begins with the story of mankind. Jesus was the Son of Adam, the Son of God. To follow the story of Jesus we must begin with the first page of the Bible. Indeed, John, in the introduction to his Gospel, takes us back even further: "In the beginning was the Word, and the Word was with God, and the Word was God." John testifies that Jesus is the Alpha and the Omega, the First and the Last, the Creator and the Goal of all history (Rev. 22:13,16). John came to this astonishing conclusion about Jesus not simply from the words and deeds that he witnessed, but because he came to recognize Jesus as the Lord of the promise, the Savior of Israel.

John starts his Gospel with "In the beginning . . ." to

point us back to the real start of the story. He writes so that we may believe that Jesus is the Christ, the Son of God (Jn. 20:31). To understand what John means, we need to examine something that he knew well: the story of the Old Testament.

Anyone who has had Bible stories read to him as a child knows that there are great stories in the Bible. But it is possible to know Bible stories, yet miss *the* Bible story. The Bible is much more than William How stated: "a golden casket where gems of truth are stored." It is more than a bewildering collection of oracles, proverbs, poems, architectural directions, annals, and prophecies. The Bible has a story line. It traces an unfolding drama. The story follows the history of Israel, but it does not begin there, nor does it contain what you would expect in a national history. The narrative does not pay tribute to Israel. Rather, it regularly condemns Israel and justifies God's severest judgments.

The story is God's story. It describes His work to rescue rebels from their folly, guilt, and ruin. And in His rescue operation, God always takes the initiative. When the apostle Paul reflects on the drama of God's saving work, he says in awe, "For from him and through him and to him are all things. To him be the glory forever! Amen" (Ro. 11:36).

Only God's revelation could maintain a drama that stretches over thousands of years as though they were days or hours. Only God's revelation can build a story where the end is anticipated from the beginning, and where the guiding principle is not chance or fate, but promise. Human authors may build fiction around a plot they have devised, but only God can shape history to a real and ultimate purpose. The purpose of God from the beginning centers on His Son: "He is the image of the invisible God, the firstborn over all creation. For by him all things were created: things in heaven and on earth, visible and invisible. . . . All things were created by him and for him" (Col. 1:15-16).

God's creation is *by* His Son and *for* His Son; in the same way His plan of salvation begins and ends in Christ. Even before Adam and Eve were sent out of Eden, God announced His purpose. He would send His Son into the world to bring salvation (Gen. 3:15).

God did not accomplish His purpose all at once. He did not send Christ to be born of Eve by the gates of Eden, nor did He inscribe the whole Bible on the tablets of stone given to Moses at Sinai. Rather, God showed Himself to be the Lord of times and seasons (Acts 1:7). The story of God's saving work is framed in epochs, in periods of history that God determines by His word of promise. God created by His word of power. He spoke and it was done; He commanded and it stood fast. God said, "Let there be light," and there was light. In the same way God spoke His word of promise. That word has no less power because it is spoken in the future tense. God's promises are sure; they will be fulfilled at the appointed time (Gen. 21:2).

Yet while the story is God's story, and salvation is His work, men and women are not just spectators. To be sure, there are times when God's people are told to stand still and see the deliverance of the Lord (Ex. 14:13-14). But they are also commanded by God to leave their homes and become pilgrims, to march through waterless wastes, and to fight hostile nations. The grace of God in delivering and leading them calls them to faith in Him, to the commitment of whole-hearted trust. Because God promises what He will do, His people may joyfully confess that "salvation comes from the LORD" (Jon. 2:9). But since God does not do all that He has promised at once, the faith of His people is tried and tested. Their longing becomes intense. At times the promise seems not only distant but illusory. They fall victim to unbelief and cry, "Is the LORD among us or not?" (Ex. 17:7).

The writers of the New Testament remind us of the reality and intensity of the faith of the Old Testament saints. The author of Hebrews surveys their tortures and triumphs, and concludes, "These all died in faith, not having received the promises, but having seen them afar off, and were persuaded of them, and embraced them" (Heb. 11:13, KJV).

To encourage and strengthen His suffering saints, the Lord often repeated His promises. Through the prophets, God spoke to Israel, denouncing the sin of those who rebelled, but painting ever more marvelous pictures of the blessing to come. The apostle Peter reflected on the ministry of those Old Testament prophets: "Concerning this salvation, the prophets, who spoke of the grace that was to come to you, searched intently and with the greatest care, trying to find out the time and the circumstances to which the Spirit of Christ in them was pointing when he predicted the sufferings of Christ and the glories that would follow" (1 Pet. 1:10-11). Not only the prophets, Peter tells us, but even the angels of heaven longed to peer into the mysteries of God's great plan.

God's drama is not a fiction in its slow unfolding, or in its staggering realization. The story of the Bible is real history, wrought in the lives of hundreds and thousands of human beings. In a world where death reigned, they endured, trusting the faithfulness of God's promise. If we forget the story line of the Old Testament, we will also miss the witness of their faith. That omission cuts the heart out of the Bible. Sunday school stories are then told as tamer versions of the Sunday comics, where Samson substitutes for Superman. David's meeting with Goliath then dissolves into an ancient Hebrew version of Jack the Giant Killer.

No, David is not a brave little boy who isn't afraid of the big bad giant. He is the Lord's anointed, chosen of God to be the king and deliverer of Israel. God chose David as a king after His own heart in order to prepare the way for David's great Son, our Deliverer and Champion. David's reply to the taunts of Goliath shows us that David was a warrior of faith: "You come against me with sword and spear and javelin, but I come against you in the name of the LORD Almighty, the God of the armies of Israel, whom you have defied" (1 Sam. 17:45).

Because David fought in the name of the Lord, his ordeal and victory had meaning beyond the immediate battle. He was confident of victory because he knew that God had called Israel to be His people. He was the God of the hosts of heaven, but also the God of the armies of Israel.

David had been anointed by Samuel the prophet. He knew that the Lord had called him from following his father's sheep to become the shepherd of Israel. David filled a role. God granted deliverance through him, not because he was brave or a dead shot with the sling, but because he was chosen, and filled with God's Spirit. When God later promised to give a Son of David everlasting rule, He made it clear that David's kingship was not an end in itself, but served to prepare for the great King to come.

In this way the Old Testament gives us types that foreshadow the New Testament fulfillment. A type is a form of analogy that is distinctive to the Bible. Like all analogies, a type combines identity and difference. David and Christ were both given kingly power and rule. In spite of the vast differences between David's royalty and Christ's, there are points of formal identity that make the comparison meaningful.

Yet it is just this degree of difference that makes biblical types distinctive. The promises of God in the Bible do not offer a return to a golden age of the past. David's Son to come is not simply another David. Rather, He is so much greater that David can speak of Him as Lord (Ps. 110:1). The scriptural scholars of Jesus' day did not understand this.

They could not answer the question of Jesus: "If then David calls him 'Lord,' how can he be his son?" (Mt. 22:45). Both Jesus and His adversaries knew that the promised Messiah was to be the Son of David. But only Jesus understood why David in the Spirit had called Him "Lord."

The story of Jesus, then, does not begin with the fulfillment of the promise, but with the promise itself, and with the acts of God that accompanied His word. As we go back to the beginning of the story, we find much that the New Testament does not tell us, because we have already been told. As we see the judges that God raised up to deliver Israel from their oppressors, we understand better what God meant when He said He would put on righteousness for a breastplate, and salvation for a helmet, and would Himself be the Judge and Savior of His people (Is. 59:16-17). When God reduced Gideon's army to a mere three hundred men, we recognize that it was God who delivered, not the strength of arms. When God reduced the force of Israel still further to one man, Samson, we see that God could deliver by one champion whose victories in life were crowned by his conquest in death.

At the same time, when we move back toward the beginning of the story, we find that the differences are overwhelming: not only for us, but for those who in faith received the promises. Samson's role as a judge pointed forward to God's promised deliverance of Israel from all their enemies, but Samson's performance fell far short of his calling. Indeed, Samson was made a judge almost in spite of himself. His deliverances sometimes came from plights of his own making as he pursued Philistine women more than Philistine armies.

Yet, blinded and mocked in the temple of Dagon, Samson nevertheless died as a judge, endued by the Lord. He stood with his hands thrust against the pillars of the temple, pillars that rested in stone sockets. Then he prayed with bitter irony for revenge against the Philistines, even though his last word was "Let me die with the Philistines!" In his death, the sacred writer tells us, he destroyed more than in his life. Here Scripture shows us that God can work His deliverance even through the death of His mighty judge.

The failures and sins of Samson, no less than his victories, are part of the story, for they show that one greater than Samson had to come if God's promises were to be realized. Samson kept only the outward purity of the Nazirite vow (and broke even that at last); true and inward purity would appear in the final Judge of Israel.

The purpose of this book is not to tell the whole story from the beginning. There is a Book that does that! Rather, its aim is to follow the line of the plot, to touch on key episodes, and to offer a guide to the underlying story of all the stories, so that we may see the Lord of the Word in the Word of the Lord.

1

THE NEW MAN

The very first written Scripture came from the hand of God Himself: God inscribed His law on two tablets of stone (Ex. 31:18). That inscription begins: "I am the LORD your God . . ." (Ex. 20:2).

God identified Himself there on Mount Sinai as the God of Israel. Israel's God was not a tribal deity, however. He was also the King of the nations and the God of creation. Included in God's revelation to Israel was not only the law by which their life and worship was to be regulated, but much more. To know the Lord their God, Israel had to know Him as the Creator. To know their calling, the people needed to know the story of their father Abraham, and his calling. It was also essential for them to know God's rule over the nations: the nations that were to be blessed through the new nation begun from the son of Abraham.

The first book of Moses begins at the beginning to tell the story that leads to the calling of Israel and their exodus from Egypt. It is the book of "generations," tracing not only the stories of the fathers of Israel, but putting their calling in the context of God's dealings with the whole human race from the time of creation. Although *all* the earth was His, Israel was God's chosen people, His precious possession. Yet Israel's calling was not for their sake alone. They were chosen from the nations, that they might bear witness to the nations. To do that, Israel needed to confess the God who called Abraham, spared Noah, and put Adam in the garden.

Made as the Image of God

"God created man in his own image, in the image of God he created him; male and female he created them" (Gen. 1:27). In a beautifully crafted literary form, the first chapter of Genesis leads up to the climax of creation: God made man and woman in His image. All the mythology of the nations is swept aside. Mankind does not originate in a process of divine copulation or from the blood of a slaughtered god. A man is not a piece of a god, nor a piecing together of god and beast. Rather, Adam and Eve are God's creatures, but creatures who bear His likeness. That they are God's creatures is perfectly clear. Their creation is not assigned to a separate day in the divine work: animals and men are alike made on the sixth day of creation.

If the first pair are blessed and told to be fruitful and multiply, so are the fish of the sea (Gen. 1:22,28). Both are multiplying creatures. Human creatureliness is further stressed when the second chapter goes on to describe the "generations" of the heavens and of the earth: that is, what God's hand brings forth from His created world. The earth brings forth living creatures at God's command, but man, too, comes from the earth. God forms Adam from the dust of the ground, and Eve is formed from the body of Adam.

On the other hand, both chapters emphasize the distinc‌-

tiveness of this human creature. In chapter one, the creation of man follows a divine determination: "Let us make man in our image, in our likeness. . ." (Gen. 1:26). The mention of the Spirit of God at the beginning of the chapter suggests that here God takes counsel with Himself, not merely as a man might address his own soul, but in the mysterious richness of the divine being. In the second chapter, the remarkable distinctiveness of the creation of man is shown first in the special care God uses to form man from the dust. Beyond the touch of God's hands is the breath of His lips. In a picture of intimate fellowship, God breathes into man's nostrils the breath of life.

Man is a creature, because he is made by God. But he is a unique creature, because he is made like God. The term "image" is used later in the Old Testament to describe idols. God forbids men to make images for worship, even images of men made in God's image. Man is made, not simply *in* the image of God, as though the divine image were reproduced in man, but rather, man is made *as* the image of God. He is like God.

Again the Genesis account is set against the convictions of the nations. Racial mythologies separate one tribe or people as descended from the gods. Royal myths teach that the king alone is made in the image of the god. A cuneiform text declares, "The father of the king, my lord, was the image of Bel, and the king, my lord, is the image of Bel."[1] In Genesis, however, *mankind* is created in the image of God, "in the image of God he created him; male and female he created them" (Gen. 1:27).

Made in God's image, man's nature and role are unique in creation. The fact that man shares organic, bodily life with all the animate creation qualifies him to represent that creation before God. Through man the praises of the physical creation can be addressed to God. Humanity, the climax of creation, has a role to fulfill. Man mediates between the Creator and the created world of which he is part. In man God may deal with His creation personally. God speaks to man, and with human lips man replies for the creation of which he is head.

Because man represents the very glory of God in created form, he also rules over creation. Man's image-bearing is joined to his dominion over creation (Gen. 1:26-27). The charming story of Adam's naming of the animals is not given just for the delight of children. It indicates Adam's calling by God to understand the forms of creation and to order them. It therefore also dramatically shows that no animal, however loyal in his service of man, can be his partner and equal.

We all know a relationship in which one differs from another, yet shows a remarkable likeness. We often say that a little boy is the very image of his father. Scripture states that when Seth was born to Adam and Eve, Adam "begat a son in his own likeness, after his image" (Gen. 5:3, KJV). Since this is recorded after the fall into sin, and since the chapter reaffirms Adam's creation in the image of God, some have concluded that the image was lost in the Fall, and that what remains is no longer the image of God but only the weak reflection of that image in Adam. In the same book of Genesis, however, the value of human life is established by appeal to the creation of man in the image of God (Gen. 9:6; cf. Jas. 3:9).

Since the image of God in some sense continues to distinguish man from the animals, we may assume that Seth in Adam's image is also in God's image. For this reason Luke traces the genealogy of Christ to Seth, the son of Adam, the son of God. The emphasis in Genesis is on the continuity of the image, in spite of the Fall. Seth, the son, is in the image of his father, and Adam is in the image of God. The implication that Luke draws attention to is clear: Adam, as the image-bearer in the likeness of God, may be called the son of God. At the same time, in Genesis it is Seth, not Cain, who is said to bear the image of his father, Adam. It is to the line of Seth, not of Cain, that God's promise is given; in that line true Sonship will be realized.

What a splendid figure is Adam in the Genesis account! Formed by God and made like God, he is placed in the garden that God planted, teeming with the richness of created life: scurrying animals, trees burdened with fruit, skies bright with sunshine or heavy with mist. This first man is the lord of all; through him creation lifts its eyes to the Creator and speaks God's praise. Adam is the cultivator of the garden, free to explore its riches and develop the world beyond. There is gold in Havilah. Great rivers water the garden and flow forth beyond it.

Adam's freedom would seem to have only one restraint. God pointed out to him one tree in the garden of which he must not eat. A smaller limitation would be hard to imagine. All the fruits of Eden were his to enjoy. All the trees were his to cultivate, all the animals his to call and command. Yet Adam, the son of God, was being tested in his obedience to his Father and Creator. He, the first man, held the destiny of all his descendants, for his was the pivotal role. He was the father of those to be born in his image; he represented the race of those who would come from him. By obedience under testing, his righteousness would pass beyond its original innocence. He would know the difference between good and evil by choosing the good. He would be confirmed as the righteous son of God, free to eat of the tree of life forever.

But Adam was alone in paradise. God formed from his very side a woman to be with him, his companion and helper. To Adam's role as head of creation was added a new role of headship in relation to the woman who was bone of his bone and flesh of his flesh. Together they could be fruitful and fill the earth that was theirs to possess.

Even before we are told the story of the Fall, the Genesis account prepares us for the role Jesus Christ would play in God's plan of salvation. The figure of Adam at the dawn of human history reminds us that God deals with mankind personally. Adam served as the representative man. Christ came as the second Adam (Ro. 5:12-21; 1 Cor. 15:22)—not as a divine afterthought, but as the One chosen from the foundation of the world to manifest all that the divine image in man may mean.

Before the story of redemption begins, the sole figure of Adam, God's image-bearer, stands before us. He receives God's command and promise even before Eve has been given to him. All this has meaning, not only for the beginning of human history, but for its culmination. Adam, the representative man, prepares us for Christ. Christ is more than a substitute for Adam, a stand-in, as it were, to succeed where Adam failed. Christ, who is the Omega, the goal of human history and of created humanity, is also the Alpha, the *true* Adam, Head of the new and true humanity. He is "the image of the invisible God, the firstborn over all creation" (Col. 1:15), for He is not only the Prince of creation; He is also the Creator. His image-bearing infinitely exceeds that of Adam, for as the eternal Son, He is one with the Father. At the last, Adam's created sonship can only reflect the greater Sonship of the divine model. The apostle Paul rejoices that the sonship we gain in Christ far exceeds what we lost in Adam (Ro. 8:14-17).

For that reason, too, God forbade the people of Israel to make images of God to focus their worship (Dt. 4:15-24). They were warned not only against the worship of idols representing other gods. They were also reminded that they saw no form when God spoke from Sinai, and that they were not to attempt to make a representation of the true God.

This does not mean that there can *be* no representation of God; after all, God made man in His image. But it means that man is not free to invent an image for worship, not even a replica of the image God made: man himself. In the plan of the tabernacle given to Israel in the wilderness, the ark of the covenant represented the very throne of God. The golden lid of this ark was the mercy-seat, the place where God was enthroned in the midst of Israel. Representations of the cherubim with outstretched wings attended the throne. But on the throne there was no image. Only the light of the Shekinah glory represented the presence of God for Israel.

Does this seem strange? God makes man in His image, but man may not replicate that image as the center of his worship. Of course, Israel had to be taught that God is an invisible Spirit, not a material being. But there was a further reason. God claimed a monopoly on His own self-revelation. He would appear to men as He chose, not as they might imagine. The empty seat above the ark was reserved for the One who was to come.

When Philip said to Jesus, "Lord, show us the Father and that will be enough for us," Jesus replied, "Don't you know me, Philip, even after I have been among you such a long time? Anyone who has seen me has seen the Father. How can you say, 'Show us the Father'? Don't you believe that I am in the Father, and that the Father is in me?" (Jn. 14:8-10).

Jesus did not refuse the worship of Mary as she anointed Him before His death (Jn. 12:1-8). It is not idolatry to call Jesus "Lord." Indeed, Christians are those who call upon the name of Jesus the Lord in their worship (1 Cor. 1:2). They recognize that there is One who bears God's image in human flesh and at whose feet we may fall down to worship (Col. 2:9; Rev. 1:17). Whoever honors the Son, honors the Father. John writes of Jesus Christ, "He is the true God and eternal life. Dear children, keep yourselves from idols" (1 Jn. 5:20-21).

Adam stands as a figure pointing us to Jesus Christ. The New Testament also perceives figurative meaning in the story of the forming of Eve. The apostle Paul goes back to the creation account to teach the right relationship of husbands and wives. Since Eve was taken from the body of Adam, he was to care for her as for his own flesh. The beautiful creation story teaches not only that marriage is a union of two who become one, but that the two were *made* of one. They belong together. But when Paul writes about this in his Epistle to the Ephesians, he does not simply talk about Adam and Eve. He passes at once to talk about Christ and the church:

> He who loves his wife loves himself. After all, no one ever hated his own body, but he feeds and cares for it, just as Christ does the church—for we are members of his body. "For this reason a man will leave his father and mother and be united to his wife, and the two will become one flesh." This is a profound mystery—but I am talking about Christ and the church. (Eph. 5:28-33)

Paul cites the command from Genesis, but he applies it to husbands and wives precisely because it deals with Christ and the church. Is Paul simply creating an allegory, an imaginative but artificial analogy, or is there a deeper connection? Can the foundation of marriage in the creation account be a type of the relation of Christ and the church? Yes, because the principle respecting marriage enunciated in Genesis 2:20-25 is fulfilled in Christ. The bond of intimate union created in marriage is to take precedence over the bonds that join us to others. A man is to leave his father and mother to be united to his wife.

In Genesis the command follows the statement of Adam ("bone of my bones and flesh of my flesh"). God's command is grounded in His act of creation. The relation of man and wife is exclusive. The love that joins them is necessarily a jealous love; that is, it is a focused love that would be broken by adultery. This principle is again stated in the Ten Commandments, when God gives His covenant law to His redeemed people. That commandment, "Thou shalt not commit adultery," is not given simply to provide a stable home life for Israelite society. It is given to define a special and intensive love that goes beyond the command to love one's neighbor.

This is the principle that God Himself invokes as He reveals Himself to Israel. God is a jealous God; His name is "Jealous" (Ex. 34:14). He demands of Israel exclusive devotion, the jealous love for which marriage is a type and symbol. His people are to love Him with all their heart, soul, strength, and mind.

Throughout the history of Israel, the people were guilty of spiritual adultery. Consider Solomon, the magnificent king at the peak of Israel's power and blessing. He built the Temple of stone and cedar and overlaid it with gold. He dedicated this Temple to the service of the Lord, praying that through all the earth people might turn to the Temple to pray, and that God would hear them.

But now we see Solomon ascending the Mount of Olives, immediately to the east of the Temple mount. He is choosing a site for a shrine to be built on the top of the mountain. There Solomon stands: he can see the glittering gold of the Temple of the Lord in the sunshine, but he is now preparing for the dedication of a shrine to Chemosh, the god of the Moabites. Solomon has come to this place by a policy of statesmanship that is full of worldly wisdom, but empty of faith. He has bought security for Israel by making treaties with the surrounding nations and sealing them in marital alliances. He builds the shrine of Chemosh, not for himself, but for one of his Moabite wives. Yet how directly and brazenly does he defy the law of God and the jealous God of Israel, who had warned His people to destroy all the altars of Canaan, "For thou shalt worship no other god: for [Yahweh], whose name is Jealous, is a jealous God" (Ex. 34:14, KJV).

But God withholds His judgment and calls Israel to repentance. Through the prophet Hosea He shows the wonder of divine love toward the adulterous wife. Nevertheless, eventually the judgment of the Lord must fall upon impenitent Israel.

When Jesus came to gather to Himself the people of God, He revealed Himself as the Bridegroom, come to claim His church as His bride. The figure is not accidental. It is not that God looks down from heaven to discern some human relationship that might prove to be a fitting symbol of His love. The reality is the other way around. When God formed Eve from the body of Adam, He was providing the means by which we might be prepared to understand the joy of an exclusive love. Only in that way could we be prepared to grasp something of the burning intensity of the divine love: love that can bear no rival, because God is a personal God, and His love for His people is personal.

Most of the religions of the world could build a shrine to Chemosh with little difficulty. Polytheistic religion can always add one more god. In pantheism, god is everything, so Chemosh is just another name for the infinite spirit. In Hinduism, Brahma is the impersonal absolute, and Chemosh could be added as just another part of a polytheistic phase that eases the path for those who are not yet prepared to take the mountain straight. Even deism, with its conception of a remote creator, may reason that he can be approached in many forms. Certainly that distant deity would not be troubled with jealousy if we called him Chemosh, or worshiped Chemosh in his absence.

The exclusive bond between God and His people is a major theme of the Old Testament, but it comes to full expression in the New. "There is no other name under heaven given to men by which we must be saved" (Acts 4:12). "Jealousy" and "zeal" are two translations of a single word in both Hebrew and Greek. The holy zeal of God burns within the mystery of the Trinity. The zeal of the Son for His Father is matched by the zeal of the Father for His Son.

When Jesus cleansed the Temple of the hucksters who had turned it into a market, He displayed His zeal for the holiness of God's house, but also for the blessedness of God's house as the house of prayer for all nations. Jesus was zealous for the redeeming grace of God symbolized by the Temple. That zeal caused Him not only to lift the scourge, but to bare His back to the scourge. Only by the zeal of His love could the jealous love of the Father for His people be satisfied. His zeal for God's house consumed Him, even on the cross. "Destroy this temple," He said, speaking of His body, "and in three days I will raise it up" (Jn. 2:17,19, KJV). It is the zeal of God's love in Christ that claims the church as the bride of the Lord.

Proven as the Son of God

When the Bible sets Adam before us at the beginning of the record given to God's redeemed people, we are already pointed to the second Adam who is to come. In the forming of Eve, and in the love of Adam for Eve as bone of his bones and flesh of his flesh, Christ is also revealed in His jealous love for the church. The apostle Paul shares that love of Christ: "I am jealous for you with a godly jealousy. I promised you to one husband, to Christ, so that I might present you as a pure virgin to him" (2 Cor. 11:2).

Adam's test in the garden points toward the testing of Christ, although Adam's disobedience turns the parallel into contrast. Matthew, Mark, and Luke all speak of Christ's temptation in the wilderness. In the Gospel accounts of the temptation, there is an underlying reference to Adam's testing in the garden.

Christ's testing came at the very outset of His ministry. It was the Holy Spirit who drove Christ into the desert: the Spirit of the Father who came upon Him at His baptism—the Spirit, therefore, of His Sonship. "Thou art my beloved Son; in thee I am well pleased" (Lk. 3:22, KJV). Adam was tested that he might be confirmed in his sonship. Jesus was tested in sonship, too. He was tested as the Messianic Son who was also the only begotten and beloved Son of the Father: the divine Son in human flesh. His encounter with Satan was a trial by ordeal. Christ invaded the fallen world where Satan was laying claim to the kingdoms of men. There He met the "prince of this world" in combat.

Just as we should see how Genesis points us to the Gospels, so we should appreciate, too, how the Gospels point us to Genesis. Christ's temptation was not endured primarily in order to give us an example of how we should deal with temptation. The temptations Satan used to assault Jesus were surely not the temptations he would use for already fallen sinners.

Certainly Satan does not find it necessary to offer all the kingdoms of the world to the average sinner. He can buy most sinners for small change. Nor does Satan tempt us to test our powers to work miracles. No, Satan's temptations of Jesus were directed at His consciousness that He was the divine Son, and that He had come to do His Father's will. Satan aimed to cause Jesus to doubt the goodness of God.

With that same aim he tempted Eve: "Did God really say, 'You must not eat from any tree in the garden'?" (Gen. 3:1). He grotesquely exaggerated the divine prohibition in Eden to insinuate that God was incredibly uncaring about human needs, and hostile to human progress.

In the wilderness, it might seem that Satan would have a much easier task. Eve and Adam lacked nothing; Jesus was in the last stages of starvation. God had put Adam and Eve in the garden; He drove Jesus into the wilderness. Yet Satan did not approach Christ nearly so directly. He did not say, "Did God really drive You out into this barren wasteland to let You die here?"

Rather, he only suggested that Christ provide for Himself, since it would seem that His Father was not providing for Him. At the same time, Satan suggested that by providing for Himself, Jesus could clear up any doubts about His own identity. Jesus had heard the voice from heaven declare that He was the Son of God. Satan would have Him question that word. "Hath God said?" echoed in the wilderness from the voice of the serpent in the garden.

Jesus repulsed that temptation by using the Word of God, quoted from Deuteronomy. Jesus not only filled the role of the second Adam, the true Son of God. He was also the true Israel, God's Son. Israel, too, had been tested in sonship after God had said to Pharaoh, "Let my son go, that he may serve me" (Ex. 4:23, KJV). God led the people of Israel in the desert for forty years, to prove them, to see if they would learn that man does not live by bread alone, but by every word that proceeds from the mouth of God (Dt. 8:2-3). God's words to Israel were given from Sinai in the Ten Commandments; they were also given to guide the march of Israel, as they struck camp or pitched their tents at the word of the Lord (Ex. 17:1).

What the people of Israel failed to do, Jesus did. In their

hunger, they failed to trust the word of God. They not only doubted God's goodness; they defied it, and despised the manna of His provision. But Jesus, in contrast to both Adam and Israel, was obedient as the true Son of God. He lived by the word of God: not only the scriptural precept, but His Father's voice from heaven, and the will of the Father that drove Him into the wilderness.

After his first temptation failed, Satan took Jesus to the pinnacle of the Temple and urged Him to cast Himself down. That temptation invited Jesus to exchange faith for sight. It had more force than we might recognize, for Satan quoted a psalm that clearly contained God's promise to His Messiah (Ps. 91:11-12). Jesus shaped His life as the one in whom the Scriptures were fulfilled. Satan was now asking Jesus not to disobey Scripture, but to fulfill it. Actually Satan was proposing presumption in the name of faith, but he was suggesting that Jesus would lack faith if He refused to put God to the test. Surely, if He did *not* jump, it must be because He couldn't believe that the angels would lift Him up before He struck the pavement of the Temple below.

Of course, there is a notable contrast between this temptation and the proposal that Eve eat of the forbidden fruit. In the garden, Satan had directly contradicted the word of God: "You will not surely die" (Gen. 3:4). But in speaking to Jesus, Satan, far from contradicting the word of God, appears to be calling Jesus to believe it and to act on it. But it is not faith to demand that God show, once and for all, whether His promises are true. This is not to receive the testing that God sends; it is rather to put God to the test.

Adam and Eve tempted God by daring Him, as it were, to carry out His threatened punishment for disobedience. Satan wanted Christ to challenge God's faithfulness in a much less direct way, but he wanted Him to act on doubt of the same kind. There would be no other reason to leap from the Temple roof except to determine, once and for all, whether God would keep His promise. To Eve, Satan essentially said, "Eat, you will not surely die—for God has lied to you." To Christ he said, "Jump, You will not surely die—*unless* God has lied to You."

Satan had one more temptation, presented as the last in the Gospel of Matthew. He took Jesus to a high mountain, showed Him all the kingdoms of the world in their glory, and promised to make Jesus king over them all—*if* He would fall down and worship Satan as the one authorized to give them away. Again, the parallel with the temptation in the garden is striking. Adam had been given dominion over the world by God: it was his legitimate calling. Yet Satan suggested that a greater dominion was possible, one in which the royalty of Adam and Eve would take on a different character, a glory they could barely imagine. They could become as God: not innocent little creatures put to digging in God's walled-in garden, but mighty rivals to God Himself, having the knowledge that God Himself possesses of good and evil.

As Satan would have it, God was not to be worshiped, but envied; not served, but thwarted. Man could be his own god, build his own dominion, possess the world not as God's steward but as an absolute monarch. The Tempter, of course, would create the assumption that he was the friend and advocate of man; that he intervened to deliver man from exploitation by God and to open for him the destiny he desires.

The implications of the temptation are evident, however. If Adam and Eve had not first been blinded by their own desires, they would have questioned the authority of the serpent. Who was this creature who called God a liar? What new relation would be the outcome of heeding the serpent rather than the Creator? If the serpent offered to make them rivals of God, what were his own desires? It is evident enough that Adam and Eve could not reject the word of the Lord without becoming captive to the word of the Devil. Satan did not openly ask for the homage of Adam, but that was plainly the outcome of his success. By obeying the serpent, Adam and Eve made themselves the friends of Satan and the enemies of God.

In tempting Jesus, Satan followed the same strategy, but again the issue was enlarged by the nature and calling of Jesus as the true Son of God. He was the heir of all the kingdoms of the world, and the Lord of the principalities and powers by which Satan would keep the nations in bondage to his will. To receive His proper dominion at once would obviously mean avoiding the suffering and death He knew to be the Father's calling to Him. Satan pretended that Jesus could gain His inheritance intact at the price of a brief acknowledgment of him as the Donor.

Malcolm Muggeridge suggested that if the temptation were to be enacted in the contemporary world, Satan would approach Jesus through the media, offering Him prime-time television to proclaim His message to the whole world, with one small acknowledgment. At the beginning and end of the program there would be the customary credit line: "This program has been brought to you through the courtesy of Lucifer Enterprises, Inc."

Jesus refused Satan's offer, and proceeded to demonstrate an authority that Satan had not offered: the authority to command Satan to depart. The analogy to the sin of Adam is present by total contrast. Adam desired a greater authority than God had given, and inherited shame and doom. He would be God's rival and thereby set himself against God, siding with the Enemy. Jesus desired to serve His Father, and inherited a dominion beyond the dreams of Adam or of Satan: a dominion that does not rival God's Kingdom, but that is one with His Kingdom.

At the right hand of the Father, Jesus Christ, the God-man, exercises total judgment and rule over all creation. Even before His exaltation to the Father's right hand, Jesus on earth displayed divine authority. Not only could He speak with divine power, but He could heal with divine ease. He commanded demons to depart, for He had bound the strong man, Satan, in single combat, and prevailed over him (Mt. 12:24-30).

NOTES:
1. Cited in Henri Blocher, *In the Beginning: The Opening Chapters of Genesis*, D.G. Preston, trans. (Leicester, England: InterVarsity Press, 1984), page 86.

2

THE SON OF THE WOMAN

Triumphant as the Son of the Woman

Where Adam stands at the beginning of human history, we see Jesus Christ. He is the Son, bearing the image of His Father. He overcomes in temptation, and His Sonship is proven in obedience. The lie of Satan is marvelously refuted in Him. The serpent had said to Adam and Eve, "You will be like God." They believed that lie and thus returned to the dust from which they came. Far from tasting glory with the forbidden fruit, the first pair tasted fear and shame.

But in Jesus, the promise of man's creation in the image of God is given the fulfillment of heavenly glory. It was God's will from the beginning that man should be like God, not in rebellion but in the union of Christ's Sonship. Man's creation in the image of God not only made the Incarnation possible; it was God's own design according to His purpose of the Incarnation. Adam's creation, the forming of Eve, the testing in the garden—all prepare us for Jesus Christ.

We do not know in what way God would have owned His image in man through Christ if Adam and Eve had not disobeyed. Surely Adam as an obedient son would have been brought to know the beloved Son. But we do know that human sin did not frustrate God's plan. Indeed, God's triumph through Christ over sin is so glorious that we are driven to conclude that apart from sin, such incredible love and mercy in the heart of God could never have been displayed. We can almost sympathize with Augustine, who cried out, "*Felix culpa!*" (Fortunate transgression!).

The wonder of God's victory over sin in Christ appeared immediately after the Fall. Adam and Eve were ashamed before God and before one another. They made tree leaves their screen to try to conceal their sexuality from one another and their persons from the presence of God. But the work of their hands could not restore the unity they once knew with one another, nor could their works shield them from the judgment of God. God sought them in the garden and they had to respond to the summons of His voice.

A judgment scene was instituted. God made inquiry into their transgression. But then they sought refuge behind another flimsy screen: the excuses by which they would shift the blame. Adam blamed Eve, becoming her accuser rather than her advocate. In the process he also blamed God. "The woman you put here with me—she gave me some fruit from the tree, and I ate it" (Gen. 3:12). Eve, in turn, blamed the serpent: "The serpent deceived me, and I ate."

Not repentance, but fear and evasion marked the response of the sinners in Eden. The Judge, having inquired into the case, pronounced His sentence. He began with the serpent, to whom Eve's testimony pointed; then He judged Eve, and finally Adam. What is so striking about God's judgment is its restraint and mercy. The penalty of disobedience was death, but Adam and Eve did not lie dead at the foot of the tree. The penalty would indeed be exacted: "Dust you are and to dust you will return" (Gen. 3:19). But before that dread sentence, the Lord spoke words of hope.

The serpent was judged before Eve and Adam, and the judgment on the serpent changed everything. God would turn the tables. Though Eve had made herself the friend of Satan and the enemy of God, God would reverse the situation. He would put the enmity not between God and man but between man and Satan. The sovereignty of God's word shines through the promise. Spoken in the future tense, it is nevertheless the word of God's power, the God who can give life to the dead, and call the things that are not as though they were (Ro. 4:17).

Specifically, it was the woman and the offspring of the woman who were made the enemy of Satan through the generations of conflict that were to follow. Not Adam but the future offspring of Adam would be the Enemy of Satan. The terms of the oracle do not make clear whether the promised seed of the woman would be her first son or a long line of her descendants. Adam appeared to understand that God's promise implied a fulfillment of the charge to populate the earth, for he named his wife Eve "living" as the mother of all the living (Gen. 3:20). Such a name stands in contrast to the sentence of death God had pronounced, but it was spoken not in defiance but as Adam's claim on the promise of God. Eve, too, spoke in faith when her first son was born: she had brought forth a man with the help of the Lord. (Gen. 4:1 could be translated, "I have brought forth a man: the Lord.")

God's promise went beyond a declaration of enmity between the seed of the woman and the offspring of the serpent. There would be a decisive outcome: the head of the serpent would be crushed, and the heel of the man would be wounded. The figure fits the curse on the serpent; it corresponds to man's aversion to poisonous snakes. But just as the serpent is not merely a beast of the garden but a mouthpiece for Satan, so, too, the judgment points beyond man's experience with snakebites to the ultimate fulfillment of this prophecy: the conflict and victory in which the Son of the woman would suffer, but the serpent would be crushed.

Paul supports this interpretation when he writes to Roman Christians, "The God of peace will soon crush Satan under your feet" (Ro. 16:20). Christ's victory over Satan will bring victory to the people of God: the designs of Satan will be totally thwarted. John reports the words of Jesus on the eve of Calvary: "Now is the time for judgment on this world; now the prince of this world will be driven out" (Jn. 12:31). Paul rejoices in God's triumph at the cross over all the "principalities and powers," the demonic forces of Satan's kingdom (Col. 2:15, KJV).

The supreme irony of Calvary is that Satan's apparent victory was his defeat. The book of Revelation pictures Satan not merely as a serpent but as a great red dragon, standing before that woman who is about to give birth, "so that he might devour her child the moment it was born" (Rev. 12:4). Although Satan's purpose was defeated when Jesus escaped Herod's slaughter of the children of Bethlehem, Satan appeared to achieve his purpose on Golgotha. To the jeers inspired by Satan, Jesus hung on the cross in apparent helplessness and died there.

But not only was Jesus raised from the dead and exalted to God's right hand (Rev. 12:5; Acts 2:32-33); He was victor in His very death. It was His death that atoned for sin, met the claims of the law, and brought salvation to sinners. Through Christ's death, God disarmed the principalities and powers, triumphing over them by the cross (Col. 2:15). In the shadow of the cross, Jesus could say, "Now is the judgment of this world: now shall the prince of this world be cast out" (Jn. 12:31, KJV).

Jesus prevailed by His life as well as by His death. He fulfilled the calling given to Adam. The command to Adam and Eve was to rule over the earth. Adam's rule is now exercised by Christ. As so often in the work of salvation, the fulfillment far outstrips the expectations aroused by the promise. Christ exercises a dominion far greater than that given to Adam. He is Lord, not only of this planet, but of the cosmos.

Christ's Lordship is exercised with a directness and immediacy that reflects His divine power, as well as His authority as the second Adam. He can command the wind and the sea and they obey Him. Fish fill the nets at His will; water turns to wine; a loaf of bread in His hand will feed a multitude. Because Jesus does not use technological means to manifest His mastery over creation, we can fail to appreciate how total that mastery is. We can marvel at man's technical conquest of the sea and the air, but no one is able to walk on water as Jesus did, far less ascend to the Father's throne.

Jesus also accomplishes the command to Adam that he fill the earth. Paul uses the terms of filling as well as dominion to describe the present Lordship of Jesus Christ (Eph. 1:20-23; 4:10). Jesus does not simply come to rescue man from the depths of his loss. He comes to accomplish for us the calling of our humanity. His is the perfect and final dominion of man over the cosmos. He, the second Adam, can say, "Here am I, and the children God has given me" (Heb. 2:13; Is. 8:17f).

A great multitude that no man can number are gathered from every tribe and people in the name of Jesus. He who fills all things with His power assembles the fullness of Israel and the fullness of the nations in the day of His glory (Ro. 11:12,25; Rev. 7:9). His accomplishment of Adam's calling does not make our service vain. To the contrary, only because He has fulfilled man's calling can our work be made meaningful, for our fellowship is with Him. His victory is our hope. In humility, not arrogance, we receive from the victorious Lord a renewed calling to do His will to this world.

The Chosen Seed

God's great promise stands. The "seed" of the woman will crush the head of the serpent; man's rebellion will be overruled. This promise gives meaning to the succeeding chapters of Genesis. The clause "These are the generations of . . . " marks the structure of the book, carrying us from mankind as the "generation" of heaven and earth to the descendants of Jacob, his "generation."

Look at the Genesis list of sources of "generations": heaven and earth (Gen. 2:4); Adam (5:1); Noah (6:9); the sons of Noah (10:1); Shem (11:10); Terah, the father of Abraham (11:27); Ishmael (25:12); Isaac (25:19); Esau (36:1,9); Jacob (37:2). The point of the emphasis on generations is that God has not forgotten His promise. The appointed line of the descendants of the woman must continue. Through the dark and bloody history of human sin and violence, God continues the line of the promise.

That continuing promise involves a continuing separation. The separation appears at once, for God is pleased with Abel's offering, not Cain's. In jealous rage, Cain murders his brother Abel. God's amazing forbearance is again evident, as it was in the Garden of Eden. Cain is spared, although he is driven into exile, just as Adam and Eve were driven from the garden.

The descendants of Cain are recorded. Their progress in technology and urbanization is described. But in spite of their unlocking of the potential of God's creation, they remain rebels. Metallurgy, poetry, and music are all developed, but the fruit of this culture is the hymn of Lamech: the song of the sword, celebrating the threats of the world's first militarist (Gen. 4:23-24).

Genesis does not present the line of Cain as a book of "generations." The narrative turns instead to Seth. God gives Adam and Eve another son. He raises up another tradition in humanity in distinction from the urbanized violence of the line of Cain. The name "Seth" is linked with the verb meaning to appoint, or establish. God has appointed another seed in the place of Abel (Gen. 4:25). It is this verb that is used in God's promise: "I will [*appoint*] enmity between thee and the woman, and between thy seed and her seed" (Gen. 3:15, KJV). The echo of the word supports our understanding that Eve is not simply rejoicing in having another son to replace Abel, but that it is God's promise that is at issue, and God's faithfulness that is hailed.

Division, judgment, and blessing continue through the "generation" sections of Genesis. The line of Seth is corrupted, perhaps through intermarriage with the line of Cain. Human wickedness and violence reach such a depth of degradation that God intervenes with the judgment of the great flood. That cataclysmic separation of humanity reduces the story to the generations of Noah, and of his sons. Again, the three sons are divided. God's blessing is given to Shem with remarkable fullness: God is to be praised as the God of Shem. His brother Japheth will come to dwell in the tents of Shem, presumably to share in the blessing that Shem enjoys. The generations of Shem are then followed in the account.

Division appears again as the descendants of Noah are united in the building of the city and tower of Babel. As in the days of the Cainites, the city is built, not to the glory of God but to exalt the name of man. Again God judges. To restrain the growth of totalitarian evil in a united mankind,

God brings confusion of language upon the inhabitants of the plain. The nations are divided, and this division provides the background for the record of the generations of Terah, the story of Abraham and his descendants.

Clearly, the book of Genesis provides an account of "generations" that leads from creation to the distinct identity of the descendants of Jacob in Egypt. Yet the story is not a fantastic mythology of a super-race. The people of Israel are not choice, but chosen. Their sins and failings are described with painful candor. The focus is not on the exploits of the fathers, but on the faithfulness of God, who called the fathers in order that His promise might not be void. The sweep of the vast panorama moves toward a fulfillment beyond the exodus, to a redemption that will reach the nations.

The term "seed" is ambiguous in Hebrew: it can refer to descendants as a corporate group, or to an individual descendant. Genesis does not specifically resolve that ambiguity. But as it holds before us the line of fathers and sons, it surely points to a second Adam, a Seed who is appointed like Seth, called like Noah, chosen like Shem, and made a blessing to all the earth as the Seed of Abraham.

3
THE SON OF ABRAHAM

The Oath-Bound Promise

Abram, an old man, walked in the darkness under the great trees where his tents were pitched. Although he was wealthy, he was a nomad, owning no fixed land in the country where his cattle and flocks pastured.

He came to a clearing beyond his camp and stood looking up at the splendor of heaven, the dark expanse pulsing with the glow of countless stars. His life had been long and difficult. He was a citizen of Ur in his first career, a city with great riches in the plains of Mesopotamia. But with his father he had left Ur for Haran, a place well to the north. When his father died, Abram and his nephew Lot left Haran, following the caravan routes around the Fertile Crescent to the land where his tents were now pitched.

Abram could reflect back on a further journey to Egypt that had almost ended in family disaster. Back in the land, he had resolved a bitter dispute between his herdsmen and those of Lot by offering Lot his choice of mountain or valley land for pasture. Lot had chosen the valley, and the city of Sodom. But when invading armies captured Lot, along with the residents of Sodom, Abram moved quickly. Using his considerable retinue of servants as a striking force, he rescued Lot and the rest of the captives. He could have added substantially to his own wealth by acquiring a share of the spoils he liberated, but he refused to touch any of it.

What filled Abram's thoughts as he stood gazing at the heavens? Not the memories of his battle, nor visions of the wealth he had declined. Abram was communing with God. His heart had carried one great burden for decades. He and his wife, Sarai, were childless.

The story of Abraham does not give us a full biography. It focuses where the heart of Abram was focused: on the promise of God. God had called Abram to leave his home and his father's house and to go forth to the land that He would show him. Abram was to be separated from Ur, and even from his relatives in Haran. He was to go forth, not as part of a migration of people but as the head of a single family. At the command of God, he was separated so that he might become the father of the line of the promise. God took the initiative in calling Abram as He had taken the initiative in calling Adam in the garden, or in calling Noah to build the ark for the saving of his house.

God's call to Abram contained a double promise: that He would bless Abram, and that He would make him a blessing. Both sides of the promise were related to God's pledge to make of Abram's seed a great nation. God would make Abram's name great by the fact that He would raise up a great people of his descendants. They would share the blessing that God gave to Abram, and Abram would be blessed by God's blessing to them.

Our understanding of blessing has faded with our

awareness of the presence of God. *Blessing* is the pronouncing of God's favor. It includes the gifts that God gives as the evidence of His love and favor, but blessing is more than what God gives. It is the bond of favor that joins God's people with Him.

Abram was blessed because he could call on the name of the Lord who revealed Himself to him (Gen. 12:7-8). Because he was blessed of God, he could also pray for others: the people of Sodom (Gen. 18:2-33), or of Abimelech (Gen. 20:17). Abram's being blessed is therefore the key to his being a blessing. As a friend of God, his name was made great, and he witnessed to the great name of God.

God's call to Abram set him apart in order to make a separate nation of him. But God did not forget the other nations, those generations of the sons of Noah listed in Genesis 10. In blessing Abram, God purposed to bless the nations. They would hear of the God of Abram, and be drawn to worship Him as their God in fellowship with His descendants: Japheth would dwell in the tents of Shem (Gen. 9:27).

But as Abram looked up at the stars, these promises were far from fulfillment. God had promised him a land, but he was still a nomad in the land that was to be his. God had promised to make of him a great nation, but his wife, Sarai, was still barren and her years of childbearing were well past. Yet Abram was brought out to look at the stars by God Himself, for God had appeared to him in a vision saying, "Do not be afraid, Abram. I am your shield, your very great reward" (Gen. 15:1).

Abram had heard this renewed promise, but it only deepened the agony of his heart. "O Sovereign LORD, what can you give me since I remain childless and the one who will inherit my estate is Eliezer of Damascus?" (Gen. 15:2). Although God had again spoken to Abram, were not the divine words only words, when the reality was so different? God promised not merely to give Abram a reward, but to *be* Abram's Reward. There was no greater blessing possible. God would Himself be the inheritance and portion of Abram and his seed.

The magnificence of the promise seemed lost on Abram, but God did not condemn him. Rather, God called him out under this night sky to kindle his faith. "Look up at the heavens and count the stars—if indeed you can count them. . . . So shall your offspring be" (Gen. 15:5). The God who spread forth the galaxies would multiply the seed of Abram. God's promise was sure. Abram looked up at the stars, and with the eye of faith he saw the glory of the Lord: "Abram believed in the LORD, and he credited it to him as righteousness" (Gen. 15:6).

The apostle Paul well singles out that verse to support his teaching of justification by faith. Abram had not earned God's favor by deeds of righteousness. Rather, righteousness was credited to him. He trusted, not in what he had done or could do, but in what God had said and would do. Abram's faith rose out of the darkness of his doubts and fears. But there, looking up to the stars, he believed God.

Yet, believer though he was, Abram sought further assurance. How could he *know* that he would indeed inherit the Promised Land? (Gen. 15:8). God's response was an even more overwhelming evidence of His royal grace and mercy. Abram was not judged because he asked for a sign. Instead, God instructed him to sacrifice a heifer, a goat, and a ram, together with a dove and a young pigeon. The animals were to be divided so that their half-carcasses would create two rows with a path in between. Abram spent the rest of the day driving off the birds of prey from this display of carrion.

As the sun went down, Abram sank into a deep sleep and was overcome by a dreadful cloud of darkness. God began to speak to him again. He spoke of dark tidings of exile, captivity, and slavery for Abram's offspring, yet again He declared a promise that in the fourth generation they would be brought back and would at last possess the Promised Land.

In the silence after the oracle, a fearful light burst the darkness. Searing lightning passed down the aisle formed by the divided pieces. The same terminology used in this account to describe both the darkness and the fire is used later to tell of the fire of the Lord at Sinai, where God appeared in fire and cloud (Gen. 15:12,17; Ex. 19:18; 20:18,21). The symbolism is clear from the prophecy of Jeremiah (Jer. 34:18-20). To walk between the divided parts of an animal sacrifice is an oath-taking ceremony. The oath is plainly self-maledictory in its symbolism: "If I do not keep the oath that I swear, may I be divided as this animal has been."

The wonder of this vision is that God Himself takes the oath. He swears to Abram by His own life that He will perform the word that He has promised. This divine oath seals the covenant that God makes with Abram. In that covenant He promises to destroy the wicked inhabitants of the land and to give it to Abram's descendants. The covenant focuses on the seed of Abram: the nation that God will raise up, the descendants (and the Descendant) of the promise.

The threat of the presence of the holy God fills the darkness and burns in the fire. God will not break His word. But what of the sins of Abram and of the nation to be born of him? Must they not be devoured by the very flame of judgment that God will bring upon the Amorites, when the cup of their iniquity is full? (Gen. 15:16). If God is to fulfill His oath of blessing to Abram, how can His mercy triumph over His wrath?

The answer is not fully revealed until God's darkness

shrouds Calvary. There God the Son bears the curse of His own imprecation, not because He is guilty but because He takes the place of the guilty. Such is the final cost of God's oath of grace. That mysterious oath has a dreadful solemnity. It points beyond the centuries of bondage in Egypt, beyond the gift of the Promised Land, to the day when God's pledge by His own life would be paid in blood (1 Pet. 1:18-19).

God Heightens His Promise

Abram believed God's promise. He was awed by God's oath, and by the specific description of the hardships in store for his offspring. But Abram was still childless. Ten long years had passed since he came to the land of Canaan. He was now in his eighties. The promise of God was not only delayed; it was surely impossible.

Sarai, his wife, knowing the hopelessness of her childless condition, proposed a strategy to Abram. According to the customs of the time, the child of a woman's servant might be reckoned as her own. So Sarai gave her slave Hagar to Abram in the hope that Hagar might bear the child of the promise. As a result, Hagar did become pregnant by Abram.

Abram's delight at the news was somewhat diminished, however, when Hagar pressed her advantage over her mistress. Abram was forced to support Sarai against Hagar. When Sarai treated her harshly, Hagar fled, but she was persuaded by an angel to return. Restored to the encampment, Hagar bore a son, Ishmael. Was this, then, the way in which God would fulfill His promise? It might seem so. God had intervened in Hagar's flight to command her to return and submit herself to Sarai. The name Ishmael ("God Hears") was given by the angel of the Lord to signify that God had heard Hagar's affliction.

More years went by. In Abram's ninety-ninth year God again appeared to him, establishing His covenant with wider boundaries and great promises. Since Abraham now had Ishmael as a son, Ishmael would head a nation, too. Abraham would be the father of *many* nations. He was given circumcision as a sign of the covenant (at a time when circumcision might seem to Abram a singularly inappropriate symbol, referring as it did to the fruit of procreation). God changed his name to Abraham: "Father of a Multitude." He changed Sarai's name to the royal title of Sarah, ("Princess"). God reaffirmed His covenant: He would be God to Abraham and to his seed after him. His covenant would be everlasting.

But God also promised again that Abraham would have a son by Sarah, his wife. She, too, would be a mother of nations, and royal lines would be among her offspring.

It was too much for Abraham. The newly-named "Father of a Multitude" doubled up with laughter. It had all gone on too long. Now it was ridiculous. Sarah was to bear him a son? At *her* age? A ninety-year-old woman bear a son to a man at the century mark?

The absurdity of the picture seemed to give wry satisfaction to Abraham after all these years of anxious hoping. Since he was now convinced that it couldn't happen, it was a relief to laugh. But before the Lord, Abraham composed himself. "Let Ishmael live before you!" said Abraham. (In other words, "Lord, be reasonable. After all, I do have a son—a fine lad, thirteen years old. Ishmael is miracle enough, Lord. Just make *him* the head of the promised nation. Choose him as the line of the promise. Your covenant promise is glorious, but to speak about a son of Sarah is just too much. . . .")

God's promises are always too much, and there are many who would propose that God settle for Ishmael. The miraculous in the Bible, including this story of Abraham and Sarah, is offensive to contemporary children of the so-called Enlightenment. Yes, the story is beautiful as a legend, but biologically it is really too absurd. God destroys His credibility by promising too much. Of course science *might* come close to some of God's miracles: frozen semen, *in vitro* fertilization, organ implants—modern biology might just bring it off. But before the advances of modern science, anything like that would have to be considered totally impossible.

The laughter of modern unbelief is quite different from the laughter of Abraham. Abraham was staggered by the promise, but he was genuinely grateful for Ishmael, and deeply concerned that the covenant of God might be fulfilled for his descendants. God assured Abraham that Ishmael would not be forgotten. He, too, would be blessed of God. But the line of the promise would come through the son of Sarah. And so God gave Abraham just the right name for his son to bear: Isaac—"Laughter!"

Not only did Abraham laugh: Sarah did, too. The angel of the Lord came to visit Abraham with two companions. Under the great trees of Mamre where Abraham had looked at the stars, the angelic visitants enjoyed Abraham's hospitality. Then they asked for his wife, Sarah. The Lord said to Abraham, "I will surely return to you about this time next year, and Sarah your wife will have a son" (Gen. 18:10). At this, Sarah, who was listening to the conversation in the entrance to her tent, burst into laughter. The angel of the Lord challenged her, "Why did Sarah laugh? Is any word too wonderful for God?"[1] Embarrassed, Sarah lied. "I did not laugh," she said in confusion. But the Lord wanted the truth on the record—and in her heart: "Yes, you did laugh."

God's promise, as we well know, was kept. Sarah did conceive and, at the time God promised, she bore a son. The little boy was given the name God had chosen for him: Isaac—Laughter. At the circumcision of Isaac, Sarah laughed again—not in unbelief but in incredulous joy. "God has brought me laughter," she said. "Everyone who hears about this will laugh with me. . . . Who would have said to Abraham that Sarah would nurse children?" (Gen. 21:6-7). Who indeed, but the God who promises the impossible and performs His promise!

In Isaac we hear the laughter of God's triumphant grace. He delights in fulfilling His absurd promise of blessing. The boasting infidel may need to be reminded that "he that sitteth in the heavens shall laugh," but there is a laughter of grace as well as of judgment. Sarah took God's point; she laughed!

Again we cannot miss the focus of the promise. Abraham would be blessed in his progeny; they would become great nations. But the focus was on Isaac, the son of the promise, the child who was given to show that no word of God is void of power. God made that clear when Abraham was required to send Ishmael away: "In Isaac shall thy seed be called" (Gen. 21:12, KJV). Isaac, the promised son was the beloved son. Indeed, he may be spoken of as Abraham's only son, for he was the heir of the promise.

In the fullness of time, God's promised Son was born. When the angel announced the wonderful birth to Mary, she did not laugh, but whispered in amazement: "How will this be, since I am a virgin?" The answer she received was the same one that God had given to Sarah: "No word is impossible with God!" (Lk. 1:37; Gen. 18:14).[1] Need we wonder that Jesus should say, "Abraham rejoiced to see my day: and he saw it, and was glad"? (Jn. 8:56, KJV). Abraham's strengthened faith clung to the promise, and his joy welcomed the birth of Laughter. So, too, he could look ahead to the day when all of God's promise would be fulfilled in his Seed.

The Promise Contradicted?
The life of Abraham was a pilgrimage of faith. His faith had been drawn to the point of absurdity, but he had learned that

no word of God is void of power. The test that remained for Abraham was, as we might say, beyond belief. Isaac, the son of the promise, was the living evidence of God's faithfulness. He was Laughter, the promise fulfilled, faith become sight.

But now God tested Abraham with a command that appeared to make faith utterly irrational. He commanded Abraham to offer up Isaac as a burnt offering at a place to be designated. What could God be asking? It was one thing to wait beyond all reason for the fulfillment of the promise. It was another thing, *against* all reason, to destroy with his own hand the promise that had been fulfilled. Did God not know the love that Abraham now had for Isaac? Yes, God knew: "Take your son, your only son, Isaac, whom you love, and go to the region of Moriah. Sacrifice him there as a burnt offering on one of the mountains I will tell you about" (Gen. 22:2).

No more fiery crucible for faith can be imagined. The cost to Abraham was everything. The whole burnt offering was a symbol of consecration, of offering up to God without reserve or remainder a lamb of the flock or an ox of the herd. Abraham had given up Ishmael, had sent him away at the word of the Lord. But now Abraham was asked to give up Isaac, totally and without reserve. It was not enough for Abraham to say, "I reckon all things to be loss for the sake of the Lord." No, he must suffer the loss of all things, and by his own hand he must carry out that dreadful sacrifice.

Even more than the price of love seems to be demanded of Abraham. What of the promise itself? Was not Abraham being asked to surrender even that? He was to be the "Father of a Multitude," but God was demanding the sacrifice of his only son. Did not the *command* of God destroy the *promise* of God? How could Abraham commit himself to trust the word of God when that very word appeared to be contradictory?

It was that dilemma that Satan sought to press upon

Jesus in the wilderness. If He was indeed the Son of God, sent to be the Redeemer of the world, was not God in the process of destroying that very word of promise by leading Him into the wilderness and allowing Him to die there of starvation? God's command to Jesus could not be trusted, Satan implied. God was not delivering Him from death, and might not deliver Him from death. It was time for Him to test God. If God was His Father, He had given Him only stones for bread. Let Him turn the stones into bread Himself, since God had not seen fit to do it for Him. So Abraham might have been tempted: to defy God's command, and in that way to cling to the reality of his situation rather than to the sheer word of God.

But because Abraham believed God, he did not doubt the goodness, wisdom, or faithfulness of God. We must remember that God did not ask him to murder his son, but to offer him as a sacrifice. The difference is important. In the Old Testament, it is evident that the lives of all sinful men are forfeit before God; God can require the death of any sinner. Further, the demand of God's judgment is directed against the firstborn as the representative of all. As Creator, God asked of Israel that they consecrate to Him the firstborn of their flocks and herds. As Redeemer, He asked of Israel their firstborn sons (Ex. 13:15; 22:29). In the Exodus deliverance, God claimed the firstborn sons of the Egyptians in judgment against their sins.

But Israel, too, was a sinful people. The firstborn sons of Israel were also under the threat of the angel of death. In order that the sons of Israel might not die, God provided the ordinance of the Passover lamb. The angel saw the blood of the lamb on the door-posts and passed over the Israelite household. Yet God's claim still rested in a particular way upon the firstborn son (Ex. 22:29). The Levites served God to discharge this claim, up to their full number. Beyond that, the law provided for the payment of a ransom. The firstborn would be redeemed by the sum of five shekels. He then remained with his family as one who belonged to God (Num. 3:11-13,44-51; 8:14-19).

God's claim on Isaac was consistent with His claim on all the firstborn of the progeny of Abraham. God was not commanding Abraham to commit a crime but to execute a judgment that was justly due.

Still further, all sacrifices that involved the shedding of blood carried the symbolism of expiation, of making satisfaction for sin. Abraham, too, was a sinner. How might he be acceptable to God? Should he offer the fruit of his body for the sin of his soul? (Mic. 6:7). Since God's promise of blessing to Abraham had to include redemption from sin, wasn't it necessary that there be a greater offering to pay the price of sin than the offering of lambs, bulls, and goats? If the promise of God's saving blessing was to come through the seed of Abraham, was not Isaac the sin-bearer? Was he not given of God to Abraham that Abraham might give him back to God?

Of course, as we know, it was God's purpose to provide a substitute for Isaac: a ram caught in the thicket on the mount of sacrifice. In the outcome, the event did not provide a justification for human sacrifice, but the reverse: God prohibited such sacrifices, accepting the offering of animals instead.

Yet we must not miss the meaning of the command. God can and must require of Abraham not only the dedication of all that he has and is, but also the full satisfaction due to God's holy justice. For Abraham to give the fruit of his body for the sin of his soul would not be too great a price; indeed, his own life was forfeit as a sinner, deserving death as the judgment of God. The cost of redemption is *everything*.

Indeed, even Isaac, the son of the promise, is not

enough. Isaac, too, is a sinner. The offering of one sinner for another could not be acceptable to God. A father cannot offer himself for the sin of his son, nor a son for the sin of his father. Isaac's submissiveness to Abraham's fearful action may indicate his willingness to serve his father even in death, but the death of Isaac could not atone for Abraham's sin. This, too, is part of the meaning of God's provision of the ram for the burnt offering, the symbol of a perfect Sacrifice to come.

Abraham's faith was tested when God asked him to give everything. Faith cannot be less than total. To trust in God means to look to Him alone, to find in Him all our hope, to hold nothing back, no reserve. Faith is commitment. Yet just because faith looks to God and not to ourselves, faith's giving is really a receiving. In commitment, the price faith pays is everything. But in total trust, the price is nothing. Faith looks to God, not man, as the giver.

The author of Hebrews calls attention to this side of Abraham's faith. By faith Abraham, when God tested him, offered up Isaac as a sacrifice. He who had received the promise was about to sacrifice his one and only son, even though God had said to him, "It is through Isaac that your offspring will be reckoned." Abraham reasoned that God could raise the dead; figuratively speaking, he did receive Isaac back from death (Heb. 11:17-19).

Abraham had received the promise from God. God's word could not fail. If Abraham was to give Isaac, then he also had to receive Isaac again. There is a hint of this in the Genesis narrative that the author of Hebrews is calling to our attention as he speaks of Abraham's faith in the resurrection. When Abraham came within view of Mount Moriah, he asked his servants to wait for him. It would not do to have a whole party in attendance while he was sacrificing his son! But as Abraham left them, he said, "Stay here with the donkey while I and the boy go over there. We will worship and then we will come back to you" (Gen. 22:5).

It would seem that the author of Hebrews sees faith, and not a deception, in the words of Abraham. As Abraham ascended the mount with Isaac, he was strangely confident that he would return with his son. God's promise cannot be voided. Perhaps this conviction on the part of Abraham appears, too, in the answer he gave to Isaac's heart-wrenching question. As they went up the mountain together, Isaac was carrying the wood for the sacrifice (he was evidently a strong youth, not a little boy). Abraham had the fire and the knife.

As they walked on, Isaac spoke to his father Abraham: "Father?"

"Yes, my son?"

"The fire and wood are here, but where is the lamb for the burnt offering?"

Abraham answered, "God himself will provide the lamb for the burnt offering, my son" (Gen. 2:6-8).

Abraham was not telling a lie when he answered Isaac's question, which plunged like a knife into his heart. There was ambiguity in his answer, but ambiguity that revealed faith. In the Hebrew text, Abraham's word here is literally "see." God would "see" the lamb for the burnt offering. This may mean God would choose a lamb, or God would "see to" a lamb. It is this term that Abraham used in naming the place of sacrifice "Jehovah-Jireh." The name is explained by the statement, "In the mount of the Lord it shall be seen" (Gen. 22:14, KJV) or "provided" (NIV).

Abraham's name for the place was a triumphant cry of faith. In that agonizing moment when his son had asked where the sacrificial lamb was, Abraham had flung himself upon the faithfulness of God. God would choose the lamb. He would see the sacrifice; He would look upon His chosen, the one He had provided. God had indeed seen, and now Abraham saw, too. He knew the mercy of God, and the provision God made for the redemption of Isaac and of Abraham. The cost of redemption was total, but what God required He provided. The faith of Abraham points us away from Abraham to God, to the God who sees, the God who provides.

God had a further purpose in summoning Abraham to Mount Moriah. He not only desired to test and strengthen Abraham's faith. He also desired to *inform* the faith of Abraham, to show Abraham by a symbol that God would pay the price of redemption. Abraham was shown Christ's day; he was taken to the very area where the Temple would later stand, to the very mount where the cross of Calvary would be erected. The Lamb that God would provide would take away sin by the sacrifice of Himself.

Indeed, the apostle Paul boldly uses the figure of Abraham's sacrifice to point us to the provision of the Father in heaven: "He who did not spare his own Son, but gave him up for us all—how will he not also, along with him, graciously give us all things?" (Ro. 8:32). The blood of bulls and goats cannot take away sin; Isaac, the son of the promise, cannot be made the burnt offering. At last, only one sacrifice can pay the price of sin: the sacrifice of the Beloved and Only Begotten Son of God.

Mystery shrouds mystery in the marvel of that ultimate Sacrifice, and the account in Genesis 2 points to the heart of it. God, who had provided the son to Abraham also provided the sacrifice for Abraham. God, not Abraham, paid the price of redemption. Indeed, only God *could* pay the price. He paid it, not in providing a ram or a lamb, but in providing His own Son, the Lamb of God that takes away the sin of the world (Jn. 1:29).

The mystery lies not only in the Incarnation: that the eternal Son of God took our human nature so that He might take our place on the cross. The mystery lies also in the giving of the Father. God is not a man, moved by passing emotions, subject to time and change. He is the eternal and immutable Creator. Yet, as the apostle Paul tells us, He gave what was dearest to Him for us sinners. When Paul describes the love God has for us, he turns at once to the death of Christ:

> You see, at just the right time, when we were still powerless, Christ died for the ungodly. Very rarely will anyone die for a righteous man, though for a good man someone might possibly dare to die. But God demonstrates his own love for us in this: While we were still sinners, Christ died for us. (Ro. 5:6-8)

Look again at Paul's words. Would you not expect him to write, "But *Christ* demonstrated his own love for us. . ."? It was Christ who died for us, even though we were still sinners. Surely Christ demonstrated His love for us. But Paul says of the Father what you would expect him to say of the Son.

Calvary demonstrates the love of the Father for us. How? Paul would point us back to the scene on Mount Moriah. He would remind us of the son that was called the "beloved," the only son of Abraham (Gen. 22:2). Abraham was asked not to spare his beloved son. We feel the wrench on his heart as Isaac asks, "Father, where is the lamb?" Yet Abraham walked on with Isaac, up the mount, the two of them together. So, too, Paul would remind us, the heavenly Father led His Beloved up the hill to Golgotha. When the Son, who was always pleasing to the Father, cried, "My God, my God, why have you forsaken me?" the Father paid the price in His silence.

We cannot understand how this can be; we know that we cannot think of the eternal God in merely human terms.

Yet, like Paul, John reminds us that "God so loved the world, that he gave his only begotten Son, that whosoever believeth in him should not perish, but have everlasting life" (Jn. 3:16, KJV). God did what Abraham did not have to do: He made His Son an offering for sin. We must reverently confess that for our salvation the cost to God was everything. "This is how God showed his love among us: He sent his one and only Son into the world that we might live through him. This is love: not that we loved God, but that he loved us and sent his Son as an atoning sacrifice for our sins" (1 Jn. 4:9-10).

Without the typology of Abraham's sacrifice, we could not understand the depth of meaning in the New Testament teaching about God's love in giving His Beloved. In the darkness of Calvary, the Father, too, paid the price of love.

In this supreme test of Abraham's faith, the structure of Old Testament typology again appears clearly. Faith is central because the promise is central. Abraham clings to the word of God, even though it appears to be contradictory. The grace of God is thereby revealed. God resolves the contradiction, but in so doing, He points forward to the greater mystery of His coming work of grace. The symbolism of God's dealings with Abraham can find their ultimate resolution and fulfillment only with the coming of Christ.

NOTES:
1. The Hebrew term *daba* and the Greek translation *rhema* may mean either "word" or "thing"; in the context of the power of God's word, "word" is better.

4
THE HEIR OF THE PROMISE

The Stairway from Heaven: The Promise Renewed
Under the same stars God had shown to his grandfather
Abraham, Jacob prepared to go to sleep. He was weary; the
sun had set on his long day of travel even before he climbed
to the height where he would spend the night. Yet it was not
the miles that had wearied Jacob, nor the small bag of belong-
ings that he dropped down on the hilltop. It was another
burden that could not be put down.

Jacob was an exile. He had left the tents of his father,
Isaac, in Beersheba far to the south. Would he ever see his
old blind father again? True, he had gone with Isaac's blessing; his father had sent him to Haran to find a bride among
his mother's people there (Gen. 28:2). But he had not left
Beersheba in peace. He had fled from the fury of his twin
brother, Esau. Esau was waiting only for the death of his
father, Isaac, to avenge himself with Jacob's blood.

Jacob knew well the rivalry that had made his twin his

enemy. Esau had been born first, and was therefore his father's primary heir. But Jacob could never agree to that. Even in birth, so his mother told him, Jacob had caught his brother by the heel. His mother's favorite, Jacob later used his skill as a cook to set up an outrageous deal with Esau. When his burly brother came in hungry from the hunt one day, Jacob was just taking a pot of lentil stew from the fire.

"Quick, let me have some of that red stew! I'm famished!" shouted the elder twin.

"First, sell me your birthright," was Jacob's reply.

Incredibly, Esau agreed. "Look, I'm about to die! What good is the birthright to me?" And so Esau sold his place as the firstborn son for a plate of stew. What Jacob desired above everything else was not worth one lunch to Esau.

That was long ago, but it was a day both Jacob and his mother, Rebekah, continued to remember. They remembered, too, when Isaac had announced that he was about to give Esau his blessing and convey to him the inheritance. The time of reckoning had come. Rebekah took immediate action. She was determined that Esau's bargain would be kept. Jacob must have the birthright. Isaac had sent Esau out to hunt for the wild game he loved. His blessing would be given after he enjoyed dinner with his hunter son.

On Rebekah's instructions, Jacob brought two goats from the flock. She cooked them to her husband's taste—spices could cover any lack of gamey flavor. Then Jacob impersonated Esau. He served his mother's "hunter's stew" to his blind father. Even if his voice could not be disguised, his arms at least could be made authentically hairy: Jacob wrapped them in goatskin.

The deception was successful. Isaac's suspicions were put to rest by Jacob's ready lies: of course he was Esau; he had returned so soon because God had prospered his hunt. Convinced at last by feeling Jacob's arms, Isaac pronounced on Jacob the blessing of the firstborn son, the blessing God had given to Abraham and to the line of God's promise.

Esau, when he arrived at last with the wild game he had taken, was first dismayed, then furious. His father would not, could not, withdraw the blessing he had given Jacob. That blessing included the right of Jacob to rule over Esau, his brother (Gen. 27:37). The best that Isaac could give to Esau was the promise that he would one day shake off the yoke of his brother—a promise that was not entirely reassuring in view of the rich blessing Jacob would share.

Jacob now had what he wanted, what he had deceived his father to gain. There was no doubt of it. Just before he had left Beersheba, his father, Isaac, had renewed the blessing, identifying it as the blessing of Abraham, the blessing that included the land and the line of the promise (Gen. 28:3-4). Jacob had it, but what did he have? Isaac himself had been a sojourner, a transient who moved from place to place as others claimed the wells he dug. But Jacob was now losing all claim to the land. He was leaving it. What would the blessing of Abraham mean to one who dared not reenter the land to which Abraham had been called?

Under the stars, Jacob placed a stone to serve as a headrest, gathered his cloak about him, and lay down to sleep. Then he dreamed. His was no ordinary dream. God, who spoke to the forefathers of old in various ways (Heb. 1:1), revealed Himself to Jacob. In his dream, Jacob saw a great stone stairway stretching up to heaven above.[1] Angels climbed it; other angels descended. In the midst of the angels was the Lord Himself. He descended the ladder, and then came and stood over Jacob.[2]

Jacob may well have known about the ziggurat towers that had been built in Mesopotamia, the land of his grandfather's birth. These structures, built in layers like squared-off wedding cakes, supported stone stairways that led up toward heaven. Archaeologists tell us that the steps of the stairways were too high for human use.[3] They were designed for the gods.

At the top of the ziggurat was a small shrine, at the bottom a larger temple. Apparently the shrine at the top of the ziggurat represented the heavenly dwelling of the god. (It could serve at least as a heliport reception lounge where the god touched down!) The god could then descend the great steps to visit his temple below.

We do not know, of course, whether the tower of Babel was designed in the ziggurat pattern. Did the proud builders of Babel seek to establish communication between heaven and earth on their own terms? (The later ziggurat at Larsa was called "The House of the Link between Heaven and Earth.") In any case, we are told that the builders of Babel planned a tower that would reach to heaven (Gen. 11:4). That same phrase describes the stairway of Jacob's dream (Gen. 28:12). Man's tower could not reach heaven. (The early Russian cosmonauts did not reach it, either, when they reported from their rocket that space was empty!) God did come down on the tower of Babel, but not to sanctify man's presumption. He came down to judge the earth, and to disrupt the proud unity of mankind, a unity that threatened to lock humanity under totalitarian darkness.

The stairway-tower of Jacob's dream was God's answer to the tower of Babel. The top of it did reach to heaven, for God was the builder, not man. God alone establishes communication between heaven and earth. True religion does not come from man's quest, but from God's intervention. Rebellious mankind has not sought the Lord. People seek instead to escape Him, erecting towers, temples, and idols after their own imaginations. A penetrating question cuts through all men's idolatries: "What have you done with God?"

God, who called to Adam and Eve as they hid themselves in the garden; God, who instructed Noah to build the ark; God, who called Abraham to leave his father's house—this same God took the initiative with Jacob. Paul reminds us that God chose Jacob, and not Esau, even before the twins were born (Ro. 9:10-13). Jacob had nothing to boast of; he had yet to learn to say with Paul, "For from him and through him and to him are all things. To him be the glory forever!" (Ro. 11:36).

To Jacob, fleeing from the consequences of his own deceit, God repeated the blessing of Abraham. He identified Himself as *Yahweh*, the God of Abraham and Isaac; the God of the promise, bound by the name that He would later reveal to Moses. He repeated the terms of the promise: the land, the line of descent, the blessing for all the families of the earth (Gen. 28:13-14). Above all, the Lord pledged His own presence with Jacob. The God of the past and of the future was Jacob's God in the present. He would be with him, keep him, and bring him back again to the land of the promise. "I will not leave you until I have done what I have promised you" (Gen. 28:15).

God had not come down His stairway in vain. He showed Jacob that he was not alone; He taught Jacob the real meaning of His covenant promise. "I will be your God, and you shall be my people"—this was the heart of God's commitment to His people. Yes, the promises of God were most specific. God would give to Jacob the land on which he was lying. He could feel that real estate under his cloak. And his descendants would be as numerous as the dust (a more down-to-earth figure than the stars of the sky!). They would spread to the west, east, north, and south.

But when Jacob awoke from his dream, he did not stand on the height surveying the land that stretched off in all directions. Nor did he think first of the bride that must be awaiting him in Haran if all the promises of God were to come true. Instead, he whispered, "Surely the LORD is in this place . . . . How awesome is this place! This is none other than the house of God; this is the gate of heaven" (Gen. 28:16-17). The wonder of the Promised Land was that God dwelt there. Jacob at last saw what Abraham had also learned: that there is a better country, the heavenly one (Heb. 11:14-16). How awesome is the spot that is the gate of heaven! Jacob was overwhelmed by the presence of the Lord, the Lord who came down the stairway to the place where he lay. He called the spot "Bethel"—the house of God.

In faith Jacob responded to the promise and the presence of God. He took the stone that served as his headrest and set it up as a memorial, not only to God's appearing but also to his own vow. He poured oil on the stone to symbolize his devotion, claimed God's promises one by one, and pledged his own dedication to the God of his fathers. Looking to the Lord to prosper him and to bring him back to the land, Jacob vowed to give God a tenth of everything God would give to him.

We should not be too ready to blame Jacob for bargaining with God. What he claimed was what God had promised; what he pledged was the thankful worship always due to the Lord who delivers. Jacob did not lose the awe and devotion his dream had inspired.

God did bring Jacob back to Bethel (Gen. 35:9-15). Again the Lord descended, and identified Himself as the God of Bethel: the God who had remained with Jacob as He promised and the God who would dwell with Jacob's descendants.

Jesus referred to Jacob's dream when Nathanael came to Him at the beginning of His ministry. Nathanael was brought to Jesus by Philip. As he approached, Jesus said, "Behold, an Israelite indeed, in whom is no guile!" (Jn. 1:47, RSV). Since

Jacob, whose name was changed to Israel, was notable for guile as the deceiver of his father, it would seem that Jesus was comparing Nathanael favorably with his ancient ancestor. Nathanael was amazed. "How do you know me?" he asked.

"I saw you while you were still under the fig tree before Philip called you."

Nathanael's response to this statement seems extraordinary: "Rabbi, you are the Son of God; you are the King of Israel." We must suppose that Nathanael had his reasons for remembering that time under the fig tree. He sensed that Jesus knew him indeed—in the inmost thoughts of his heart.

Jesus welcomed Nathanael's faith, and promised that he would see greater things. Addressing Nathanael and the others, Jesus said, "I tell you the truth, you shall see heaven open, and the angels of God ascending and descending on the Son of Man" (Jn. 1:51). Jesus promised a revelation that would far surpass Jacob's dream. The stairway of Jacob's dream was a symbol of the communication that God provides between heaven and earth. By that stairway angels can go up to heaven from God's presence on earth and come down to earth from God's dwelling in heaven.

The stairway was a picture in Jacob's dream. But what the dream promised became a reality in Christ's Incarnation. God came down in the person of His Son to dwell on earth. Christ is the link between earth and heaven. He is the true Bethel, the House of God, Immanuel, God with us. Jacob anointed a stone with oil to memorialize the presence of God, and called the stone the House of God. But God anointed His only Son with the Spirit.

At Bethel God confirmed His covenant with Jacob, promising never to leave him, but to give him His blessing. That blessing has been brought to us by Jesus Christ, who is present with us by means of His Spirit. As the Lord said to

Jacob, "I will never leave you," so the Lord Christ says to His disciples, "I am with you always, to the very end of the age" (Mt. 28:20). Jacob could describe his whole life as a pilgrimage (Gen. 47:9). Like Jacob, Christ's disciples are pilgrims, traveling to the city of God (Heb. 11:13; 13:14; 1 Pet. 2:11). Yet they are never alone. Every morning Christians may anoint God's Anointed with the fresh oil of devotion, and say, "This is the gate of heaven. God is in this place!"

Christ, who is the Temple of God, is also the stairway, the One in whom heaven comes down to us and through whom we ascend to heaven. Jesus spoke of His ascending and descending to Nicodemus, a member of the Jewish Sanhedrin who paid him a night visit. Nicodemus recognized that Jesus was a teacher who had come from God. He was little prepared, however, to understand the sense in which Jesus had come from God, and who He really was. Jesus' teaching about the work of the Spirit in the new birth baffled him. But if Nicodemus and the other teachers of Israel did not believe when Jesus spoke of things on earth, how would they believe when He spoke of things in heaven? "No one has ever gone into heaven except the one who came from heaven—the Son of Man, who is in heaven" (Jn. 3:13, NIV margin).

These words of Jesus to Nicodemus reflect a passage in the book of Proverbs. Agur, the author of the passage, professes to be ignorant, to lack wisdom and understanding of the Holy One. But he suggests that he is by no means alone in his ignorance: "Who has gone up to heaven and come down? . . . Who has established all the ends of the earth? What is his name, and the name of his son? Tell me if you know!" (Prov. 30:4).

Agur implies that to know God we need to have access to God: to have someone go up to heaven and bring back God's word. Jesus affirms that the One who would ascend to heaven must first come down from heaven; indeed, that coming, He must also remain in heaven, His own home (Jn. 3:13, ASV). He is the Son of Man; He will indeed ascend to heaven, but He has first come down from heaven, and can therefore speak of heavenly things. Jesus, the Son of Man, has come down so that he might be "lifted up"—first on the cross, and then to the Father's throne. One day He will come in the glory of His Father and with the holy angels; but He is already present, speaking with Nicodemus.

Jesus it is who has ascended the stairway to heaven. He can ascend because He has first come down. He can lead us up that stairway because He was lifted up on the cross. Through the cross, Jesus is the way to heaven, even as He is the truth, the full and final revelation of the presence of God. We come to the Father through Him. Heaven stands open through Him whom the angels serve.

The Ordeal of Israel: Clinging to the Promise

The Lord revealed Himself to Jacob before he left the land of the promise; Jacob knew that he was the heir of God's blessing. Twenty years later, Jacob returned to the land and again God made Himself known to the patriarch. Those two decades of exile had been years of struggle and blessing. Jacob had left as a solitary refugee; he returned as the head of two caravans. Jacob the deceiver had been deceived by his crafty uncle Laban. Yet God's blessing overwhelmed Laban's spite. Everything that Jacob touched prospered. As he journeyed back, his wealth followed him in streams of sheep, goats, and cattle.

Jacob had four wives: Rachel, whom he loved and for whom he had served Laban a total of fourteen years; Leah, Rachel's sister, whom Laban had foisted on Jacob; Bilhah, Rachel's maid, whom Rachel gave to Jacob before she had children of her own; and Zilpah, the servant Leah gave to Jacob at a time when she was not bearing children. Jacob's

twelve sons, born of these women, became the heads of the tribes of Jacob (renamed "Israel").

High drama surrounded Jacob's return to the land. He returned in obedience to God's command. His departure from Haran, however, was an unceremonious flight, a flight that did not evade Laban's pursuit. The two concluded an uneasy truce with an appeal to the Lord to oversee their separate mistrust: "May the LORD keep watch between you and me when we are away from each other. . . . Even though no one is with us, remember that God is a witness between you and me" (Gen. 31:49-50).

Escaping from his confrontation with Laban was only a small part of Jacob's concern. He knew that in returning to the land he was exposing himself to the hatred and sworn revenge of Esau. With growing apprehension Jacob approached the boundaries of the land. There he was met not by Esau but by potential adversaries of a different order. He was made aware of the presence of two companies of angels. Appearing as guardians of the land of the promise, the encamped angels offered a challenge to Jacob. He was reminded that his return was an encounter, not simply with his brother, Esau, but with the Lord of Hosts (Gen. 32:1-2). Yet the awe that Jacob must have felt before the angels brought reassurance as well. He was shown that the God of the promise kept the land of the promise. The one who knows and fears the Lord of Hosts need fear no other.

In order to make peace with Esau, Jacob sent a delegation to his brother, assuring him of his prosperity and seeking his good will. Jacob's messengers brought back no reply from Esau, but they had alarming news: Esau was on his way to meet him with four hundred men! In near panic, Jacob divided the two companies of his entourage and fled to the Lord in prayer. He reminded the Lord that he had returned at God's command, trusting His promise. He confessed, "I am unworthy of all the kindness and faithfulness you have shown your servant. . . . Save me, I pray, from the hand of my brother Esau . . ." (Gen. 32:10-11). How would Jacob's descendants become as countless as the sand of the seashore if Esau's troop obliterated the whole family?

To appease Esau, Jacob prepared a series of magnificent gifts. Goats, sheep, camels, cattle, asses—Jacob selected hundreds of animals and separated them into companies. Of the goats, sheep, and cattle, he took special care to provide not only large numbers of female animals, but enough males to serve as breeding stock. Jacob's gift was more than a present; it was an endowment. Further, Jacob took pains to see that his gifts would have maximal impact on Esau. The groups of animals were to be widely separated; the servant in charge of each was to announce the gift and say that Jacob was still to follow.

But suppose that even this caravan of presents did not mollify Esau. This was Jacob's fear. So he made one last desperate arrangement. He sent his two companies northward across the stream of the Jabbok. Jacob entered the land from the east, moving, it would seem, along the south side of the Jabbok.[4] Esau was approaching from the south. Jacob's move, therefore, put his family and flocks on the further side of the stream from the approaching troop of his brother. If Esau were to attack, he would have to cross the stream. While he fell on one company, the other might make good its escape.

Jacob remained behind as the last of the straggling sheep were moved down to the water of the ford. Yet suddenly he realized he was not alone. In the darkness he encountered another, a mysterious figure who silently grappled with him in a desperate wrestling match. In the ancient Near East, wrestling had very different associations from the buffoonery of TV bouts in our culture.[5] One way in which a legal case could be settled was by the ordeal of a wrestling match—a trial by combat.

Jacob was on trial in this struggle. All his life had been spent in conflict. In his mother's womb he had wrestled with his twin brother, Esau, and they had been in contention ever since. Jacob feared that the dawn might bring the last battle in that strife. But another, and a deeper, struggle brought this crisis in his life. Jacob's struggle was with God. Earnestly, fiercely, he had sought the blessing of God's promise. He would prevail at any cost, by any means.

The urgency of Jacob's life desire drove him against his opponent, twisting, gripping, lifting. At some point in the gasping agony of the fight, Jacob realized that this was more than mortal combat. At issue was the whole meaning of his life. The prize was the blessing that he sought; the One who struggled with him was the very Angel of the Lord—God Himself appearing as a man. No wonder Jacob felt his adversary to be too strong for him.

The pressure was too great. They were standing now, and Jacob's thighs trembled as he strained to resist. Yet his fear brought desperation. He could not yield; he must prevail. At that moment his opponent touched his hip, and Jacob felt a paralyzing shock. The strength of his leg was gone. He could not thrust with it; he could not even put his weight on it. The match was over; Jacob was lamed. Yet for Jacob the fight could not be over. Lame as he was, blinded by his tears, he clung the more fiercely to his awesome adversary. If he could not win by strength, he would prevail in weakness.

"Let me go," said the stranger. "It is daybreak."

Jacob answered, "I will not let you go unless you bless me."

"What is your name?"

"Jacob."

"Your name will no longer be Jacob, but Israel, because you have struggled with God and with men and have overcome."

Jacob said, "Please tell me your name."

But the Angel replied, "Why do you ask my name?" and then blessed him there (Gen. 32:29).

Centuries later the prophet Hosea reminded Jacob's descendants of their forefather's strange victory (Hos. 12:2-6). The tribes of Jacob—Israel in the north, Judah in the south—were alike guilty before God. Let them remember Jacob: God dealt with him amid his deceptions, but he prevailed with God as he wept and sought His grace.

Jacob's victory was not, of course, a conquest. He had not mastered the Angel of God. Lame and helpless, he could only cling to the One who had laid hold of him. His victory was a victory of faith. He did not let go because he *could* not. God's blessing was all his hope and desire. Faith wins when it knows that all is lost, and clings to God alone. "Israel," the name God gave to Jacob, reflects this ambiguity. Normally it would be taken to mean "God Prevails." But the Lord turns the meaning around as He gives the name to Jacob: Jacob has prevailed with God. In that name Jacob's desperate faith is acknowledged by the Lord.

In the morning, Jacob called the name of the place "Peniel" (the Face of God). "It is because I saw God face to face, and yet my life was spared." When the Lord had said, "Let me go, for it is daybreak," the point was that there was great danger for Jacob if, in the light of the rising sun, he was able to see the face of God. As God later said to Moses, "You cannot see my face, for no one may see me and live" (Ex. 33:20). Yet Jacob continued to hold fast to the Lord.

In the dim light of the early dawn, Jacob looked upon the face of his Maker and was spared. Later that morning, Esau came with his four hundred. He did not attack Jacob, but embraced him. Jacob urged him to keep the presents he had sent: "If I have found favor in your eyes, accept this gift from me. For to see your face is like seeing the face of God, now that you have received me favorably" (Gen. 33:10). Whatever that flattering expression conveyed to Esau, its implications for Jacob were strong. Having seen the face of God, he need not fear the face of Esau, or of any other man. The favor Jacob saw on Esau's face was favor given by God. He had been delivered, not just from the hand of Esau, as he had prayed, but from the hand of God.

In the rich historical symbolism of this account, God's revelation points us forward to Christ in a double way. In the first perspective, Christ appears in this narrative as the Lord. This manifestation is more than a symbol. The appearing of the Lord as a man or as the Angel of the covenant anticipates the Incarnation. The term "theophany" describes such appearances of the Lord. God told the nation of Israel in the wilderness that He was sending His Angel before them to keep them on the way, and to bring them to the Promised Land. "Pay attention to him and listen to what he says. Do not rebel against him; he will not forgive your rebellion, since my Name is in him" (Ex. 23:21). As the possessor of the divine Name, the Angel is the representative of God's presence, the form in which God Himself appears—distinct from the Lord, yet identified with Him.

Similar mystery surrounds this identity/distinction in other accounts of God's appearing. Abraham's three visitors at Mamre are first identified simply as men. Later, the two who go on to Sodom are said to be angels (Gen. 19:1). One remains with Abraham, and He is identified as the Lord (Gen. 18:17,22). So, too, it is the Lord Himself, who appears in order to challenge Joshua; He identifies Himself as the Captain of His armies (Josh. 5:13-14; 6:2).

At the point that a man appeared in the darkness to

wrestle with Jacob, God's revelation had gone beyond the dreams through which He had formerly communicated with him. God appeared as Jacob's opponent, yet this revelation showed His final purpose of mercy toward Jacob. In the similar situation just mentioned, Joshua saw the man with a drawn sword as an adversary, and challenged him with a soldier's directness. Moses, too, at the beginning of his mission was confronted by the threat of the Lord's power (Ex. 4:24). Yet in each case, the Lord was revealing not only His justice (the claim that His righteous judgment makes against the sinner), but also His mercy: the plan of salvation by which God would come, not in appearance only, but as true man, the incarnate Son of God.

The strange defeat of the Lord at Peniel shows the sure bond of His covenant promise. God is faithful. Jacob, weak and erring though he be, may claim the blessing God has promised. Christ the Lord would have us cleave to Him utterly. To speak of "accepting" Him is to use far too weak an expression. Like Jacob, the believer cries, "I will not let you go unless you bless me."

What a strange victory the Lord wins at Peniel! Jacob appears to be the winner in the wrestling bout. He strives with God and overcomes. The Lord cannot escape lame Jacob's grasp without bestowing the prize for which Jacob fights. Yet losing, the Lord wins. He suffers an apparent defeat to gain the true victory. The weakness of God is stronger than men. The Lord of glory humbles Himself so that helpless sinners may receive His blessing.

The name of the Lord is too wonderful for Jacob's ears; the face of the Lord is too glorious for Jacob's eyes. Yet the Lord Himself comes that Jacob may know Him. His coming to Jacob anticipated His coming to us. Jacob saw the face of the Lord but dimly; we see the light of the glory of God in the face of Jesus Christ. Jacob asked for God's own name; we are baptized into the name of the triune God. Through the name of Jesus, exalted above every name, we bear the name of the Almighty God as our heavenly Father.

There is a second way that Christ appears in this narrative. God's covenant established a relationship in which God is the Lord and we are His servants. The theophany of God's presence anticipates the coming of Christ as the Lord; the role of Jacob anticipates the coming of Christ as God's servant. Just as Jesus is the true King, fulfilling the role of kingship portrayed in David; just as Jesus is the true prophet like Moses—just so is Jesus the true Israel, who prevails with God to receive all the promises. (See Isaiah 49:3, addressed to the individual Servant; and Romans 15:8.)

Jesus was that Suffering Servant of God. The agony that He endured came about because He was smitten, struck down, afflicted by God. There is a real connection between Jacob's wrestling in the darkness of Peniel and Christ's agony in the darkness of Gethsemane. The differences between Jacob and Jesus are great, but Jesus did fulfill without sin the calling that sinful Jacob could only foreshadow.

A symbolic detail in the narrative points to this reality. Jacob was struck by the Angel on the thigh. In the Old Testament the term "thigh" is sometimes used as a euphemism for the genitals. When Abraham made his servant swear with his hand on his thigh, the symbolic gesture related the oath to the power of procreation, and therefore to Abraham's descendants (Gen. 24:2,9). Jacob's progeny, who went down with him to Egypt, are described as those who had come out of his "thigh" (Gen. 46:26; Ex.1:5).[6] The same term is used as in the account of Jacob's wrestling match. The smiting of Jacob on the thigh has reference therefore to his descendants, and prophetically points forward to the great Descendant who would bear the stroke of judgment to receive the blessing of the promise.

The prophetic detail of the smitten thigh only illumines a picture that is constant in the Old Testament. Salvation must come through the descendant of Eve, through the descendant of Shem, through the descendant of Abraham. In blessing Jacob with many descendants, God was preparing for the coming of the One. As God's servant and the heir of God's promise, Jacob points us to the *true* Israel, who prevailed in the agony of His death to bring us to God, that we may see His face.

The Promised Prince: The Blessing of Israel

The book of Genesis begins with God's creation of light and life; it ends with the embalming of a mummy in Egypt. Yet Genesis was not written as a death knell, tolling the doom of human sin. It was written to trace the hope of God's deliverance, His promise of salvation. The mummy was the body of Joseph, the son of Israel who became a prince in Egypt. His body was preserved by the arts of Egypt, but not to be entombed with the Pharaohs. Rather, Joseph's last charge to his brothers was that his body be carried with them when God would lead the Israelites out of Egypt and back to the land of the promise. Joseph shared the hope of Israel, his father: God would yet do all that He had promised to Abraham.

The story of Joseph, so beautifully told in the book of Genesis, is part of the story of Jacob, or Israel. Jacob, who had struggled to gain God's blessing, concluded his life by giving God's blessing to his sons (Gen. 49). The blessing Israel gave expressed his faith in God, and also bore witness to the blessing of salvation that God would give. "By faith Jacob, when he was dying, blessed each of Joseph's sons, and worshiped as he leaned on the top of his staff" (Heb. 11:21).

Jacob's blessing reflects some of the sorrows that he had surmounted in his earthly pilgrimage. He was already an old man when he had come to Egypt. When his son Joseph presented him to the Pharaoh, he spoke about his struggles: "The years of my pilgrimage are a hundred and thirty. My years have been few and difficult, and they do not equal the years of the pilgrimage of my fathers" (Gen. 47:9).

We might find it hard to think of Jacob's years as few, but we can freely acknowledge that they were difficult. His troubles did not end when he returned from those twenty years of service to Laban in Haran. His first attempt to settle in the land ended in disaster. He purchased a plot of ground near Shechem. He was going to set up his tents, not as a traveling nomad but as a resident rancher.

That peaceable effort ended, however, in another traumatic flight. Shechem, the ruler of the region, raped Dinah, Jacob's daughter, then sought to negotiate a marriage contract to take her as his wife. Simeon and Levi, Dinah's brothers, pretended to favor the contract, stipulating that the men of Shechem must agree to circumcision. Taking advantage of the painful aftermath of this operation, Simeon and Levi raided the town, put the men to the sword, and, with the help of their brothers, made off with the booty of the place. Jacob lamented their murderous vengeance; his blessing on them became, in part, a curse: "Simeon and Levi are brothers—their swords are weapons of violence. . . . Cursed be their anger, so fierce, and their fury, so cruel! I will scatter them in Jacob and disperse them in Israel" (Gen. 49:5,7).

The prophecy was fulfilled in ways that Jacob did not foresee. Simeon's tribe was given its inheritance within that of Judah; it was scattered and lost to view as an entity (Josh. 19:1,9). The tribe of Levi, however, rallied to the Lord's cause during the later wilderness testings of Israel (Ex. 32:25-29). Because of this, the tribe of Levi was marked out for the service of the Lord. They were scattered, indeed, but as God's ministers among the people (Josh. 13:33; 21:1-3).

The Genesis account makes it clear, however, that even the rash way that Simeon and Levi took judgment into their own hands was overruled by God for good. The marriage treaty that had been proposed by the Hivites of Shechem aimed at nothing less than the absorption of the family of Jacob into the Canaanite population. The success of such a project would have ended the distinctiveness that Israel had to preserve if they were to be a light to the nations, the channel of God's promised blessing.

Jacob's family troubles were not limited to the violent behavior of Simeon and Levi. They could be traced back to the jealousies and tensions of his polygamous household. Reuben, Jacob's firstborn son, whose mother was Leah, brought disgrace on himself by sleeping with Bilhah, the concubine of Jacob who had been the maid of Rachel. In Jacob's blessing, that sin, too, was brought to light: his words to Reuben were not so much blessing as judgment (Gen. 49:3-4; cf. 35:22).

The stern words of Jacob to Reuben, Simeon, and Levi stand in contrast with the rich blessing he gave to Joseph (Gen. 49:22-26). Jacob's joy in blessing his son Joseph reflects his gratitude to God. His loss of Joseph had been the great sorrow of his old age. When God restored Joseph to him, he knew resurrection joy. His son was, as it were, alive from the dead.

From the beginning of his days in Haran, Jacob had loved Rachel; Joseph was Rachel's son, born to her after many years of barrenness. Jacob's love for the mother drew him to her son. His favoritism was shown in the well-known "coat of many colors" that he gave Joseph.[7]

Jacob's preference for Joseph aroused the jealousy of his brothers in that divided family. Joseph, as a youth of seventeen, tended sheep with the sons of his father's concubines;

he made them furious by reporting their evil deeds to his father. What brought their hatred to the boiling point, however, was God's favor toward Joseph. Imagine their reaction when Joseph announced to them one day, "Listen to this dream I had: We were binding sheaves of grain out in the field when suddenly my sheaf rose and stood upright, while your sheaves gathered around mine and bowed down to it" (Gen. 37:6-7).

That could be topped only when Joseph said some days later, "Listen, I had another dream, and this time the sun and moon and eleven stars were bowing down to me" (Gen. 37:9). Even Jacob felt that a reprimand was in order. Would Joseph's parents indeed bow down to him? Still, Jacob did not forget the matter. He had reason to remember that God could give improbable dreams!

But if Jacob thought it possible that the Almighty had great purposes for Joseph, his hopes were shattered one day by an awful sight: the cloak of Joseph, brought to him by the brothers. Joseph was missing, they said, but they had found this cloak, torn and bloody. Could Jacob identify it? Jacob was destroyed by grief. Clearly Joseph had become the prey of the lions and vultures of the wilderness. Jacob had sent him to seek out his brothers; alone in the open country he had apparently been attacked and devoured. Where was the defense that God had given to Jacob?

In the light of what followed, Jacob could affirm God's keeping. Joseph was safe: "because of the hand of the Mighty One of Jacob, because of the Shepherd, the Rock of Israel, because of your father's God, who helps you, because of the Almighty, who blesses you . . ." (Gen. 49:24-25).

God did, indeed, keep His covenant with Israel in the life of Joseph. The psalmist reminds us that through Joseph, God provided for the family of Israel in time of famine: "He called down famine on the land and destroyed all their supplies of food; and he sent a man before them—Joseph, sold as a slave. They bruised his feet with shackles, his neck was put in irons, till what he foretold came to pass, till the word of the LORD proved him true" (Ps. 105:16-19).

To Jacob, the calamity of the famine appeared to be added to the calamity of the loss of his beloved son. Yet God used one to provide for the other. Joseph could say to his brothers, "You intended to harm me, but God intended it for good to accomplish what is now being done, the saving of many lives" (Gen. 50:20).

Jacob, too, perceived God's hand of blessing through Joseph. To Abraham, to Isaac, and to Jacob, God had promised blessing to the nations through their "seed"—a term that could refer to one descendant. Certainly God had blessed the Gentile land of Egypt through Joseph. God revealed to Joseph the meaning of the strange dreams given to Pharaoh. Through this revelation God warned the Pharaoh of the seven years of famine that would follow seven years of abundance. Perhaps the Pharaoh of Joseph's time was himself Semitic: a ruler from the Hyksos invaders who had assimilated Egyptian culture, but who used Semites in administrative positions. Even in such a setting, however, it is astonishing to see the authority the Pharaoh was willing to give to Joseph as the interpreter of his dreams. Clearly it was the Lord who raised up Joseph to rule in Egypt.

Jacob, as he blessed Joseph, was blessing the Lord, not only for delivering his son but for showing His faithfulness to the great promise that was the center of Jacob's life. God was making his descendants a nation; more than that, God had raised up a son of Israel to be a blessing to the nations, to rule in wisdom for the preservation of life.

What God did was astonishing; the way in which He did it was even more astonishing. Israel's sons did not gain control in Egypt by military or political power. They did not put Joseph on his vizier's throne. Rather, they had sought to kill their brother, precisely because of the prophetic gift that was his. Joseph had gone to Egypt, not as a prince but as a slave. Even as a slave in Egypt he had been persecuted for the sake of righteousness, the victim of the false accusations of Potiphar's wife because he would not commit adultery.

Joseph was God's righteous servant, suffering because of his faithfulness to God. Yet the path of suffering led to a throne and to the fulfillment of the word of God, given by the revelation of his dreams. God had made the life of Joseph a sign of the way in which His blessing would come. By the word of God and the servant of God, the mercy of God would be made known to the nations.

Jacob's blessing upon his sons shows his joy in what God had done. His blessing of Joseph is particularly rich. It seems surprising, therefore, that when Jacob pronounces his blessing of the ruler's scepter and the obedience of the nations, he does not apply this blessing to Joseph but to Judah. It is to Judah, not Joseph, that Jacob sees his sons bowing (Gen. 49:8). The dream that was fulfilled for Joseph, old Israel now puts in prospect for Judah. He likens Judah to a crouching lion, and continues: "The scepter will not depart from Judah, nor the ruler's staff from between his feet, until he comes to whom it belongs and the obedience of the nations is his" (Gen. 49:10).

No doubt Jacob knew of Judah's leadership among the brothers, and of the faithful way in which Judah had met the test Joseph had given them. When they came to Egypt to buy grain, they did not recognize Joseph. He accused them of being spies, and drew from them news of his full brother, Benjamin. He then pretended to make the existence of Benjamin the proof of their story, and kept Simeon as a hostage until they would bring Benjamin.

When the famine forced the brothers to return to Egypt,

Judah guaranteed his father that he would bring Benjamin safely back. That guarantee was severely tested. Joseph had his silver cup planted in Benjamin's sack of grain. He then had him pursued and arrested as a thief. The brothers did not abandon Benjamin, but returned to Egypt with their arrested brother. It was Judah who offered himself as hostage in the place of Benjamin so that the young man could be returned to his father.

This evidence of Judah's repentance overwhelmed Joseph. In tears he told his brothers, "I am Joseph!" Judah's intercession for Benjamin demonstrated as words never could the genuineness of his sorrow for the betrayal of Joseph. No doubt the repentance of Judah provided the background for the blessing he received. Yet Jacob's blessing goes far beyond anything the aged patriarch could control or understand. He spoke by inspiration: it was the purpose of God that the Messiah would come of the tribe of Judah.

Jacob's blessing assigned the rule among the tribes of Israel to Judah. Far beyond that, it spoke of the obedience of the nations being given to him. Obviously what the Lord had done through Joseph made vivid the reality of this promise. The God of Israel sent the years of plenty and of famine; He was in charge of the lives of the chief butler and the chief baker; He could raise up a slave from prison and put him on the throne of Egypt. Jacob's blessing looked forward in faith to the kingdom God would establish for His Seed, but the old patriarch's faith had surely been strengthened by the sign God had given in the life of Joseph.

Was it difficult for old Jacob, leaning on his staff, to confess again the promises of God? After all, he was again an exile. The land of Goshen in Egypt was not the land of the promise. Further, Jacob surely knew of the prophecy given to Abraham: his descendants must serve a foreign nation for four hundred years (Gen. 15:13). The blessing Jacob gave in this situation looked forward to what God would do. As Joseph had served, so must Israel serve, but in God's own time the blessing to the nations must come through the seed of Abraham. The Ruler of God's choosing would eventually come, and the scepter would be His.

The translation from the *New International Version*, "until he comes to whom it belongs," assumes that the Hebrew is to be read with different vowels from those inserted in the traditional text. Another interpretation, using the traditional vowels, would be, "until the Peacemaker comes."[8] It may be best to leave the word untranslated as a proper name: "until Shiloh comes." Whatever the difficulty of understanding that word, the thrust of the whole text is clear. The God of Israel had determined to raise up the Ruler who could bring blessing and peace to the nations.

The ancient prophecy is recalled again in the last book of the Bible. John weeps because there is no one who can open the book of God's decrees. One of the elders in the heavenly throne room responds, "Do not weep! See, the Lion of the tribe of Judah, the Root of David, has triumphed. He is able to open the scroll and its seven seals" (Rev. 5:5).

Jesus, the Lion of Judah, is also the Lamb that was slain. He who is the Lord came as the Servant. There is more than a chance similarity between the sign of Joseph and the fulfillment in Jesus. Deep in the structure of God's redemptive plan is the principle that His power is made perfect in weakness. Not by human might, but by the power of God's Spirit, the promises of His word are fulfilled. God's chosen Ruler is His Suffering Servant, betrayed by His brethren but raised up to fulfill God's promise.

NOTES:
1. The Hebrew word here applies to a rising flight of stone steps rather than to a painter's ladder.

2. Some translations interpret the text to mean that God stood above the ladder, rather than over Jacob. The Hebrew word may mean either "above it" or "beside him." The meaning is decided, however, by the similar expression in Genesis 35:13. There God appears to Jacob a second time at Bethel after his return from exile. The passage states that God, after talking with Jacob, "went up from beside him at the place where he had talked to him." The same preposition is used as in Genesis 28:13. It is clear that in both cases God came down to stand beside Jacob.

3. See André Parrot, *The Tower of Babel* (N.Y.: Philosophical Library, 1955).

4. See the article by K.A. Kitchen on "Mahanaim" in J.D. Douglas, ed., *The Illustrated Bible Dictionary*, Part 2 (Wheaton, Ill.: Tyndale House Publishers, 1980), page 936.

5. In the "Gilgamesh Epic," the hero first encounters his friend Enkidu in a furious wrestling match. The Old Babylonian account of the legend dates back to the early second millennium BC. Jacob may have known the story. James B. Pritchard, ed., *The Ancient Near East*, Vol. 1 (Princeton, N.J.: Princeton University Press, 1958, 1973), page 50.

6. "Jacob's thigh is Jacob's progeny. . . ." P.A.H. de Boer, "Genesis XXXII 23-33: Some Remarks on the Composition and Character of the Story," *Nederlandisch Theologisch Tijdschrift*, Vol. 1 (1946-1947), pages 149-163. See J. Pedersen, *Der Eid bei den Semiten* (Strassburg: 1910), page 151.

7. Another possible translation is "Long robe with sleeves." R.E. Nixon, in the article "Joseph" in *The Illustrated Bible Dictionary*, favors "multicolored." The *Dictionary* displays a color photograph of an Egyptian wall painting depicting such a robe, worn by an Asiatic caravan leader—Part 2 (Wheaton, Ill.: Tyndale House Publishers, 1980), page 813.

8. This translation is defended by E.W. Hengstenberg, *Christology of the Old Testament* (Grand Rapids: Kregel Publications, 1970), pages 30f.

5

THE LORD AND HIS SERVANT

God Keeps His Promise: The Exodus

Moses was in retirement; his years of court life in Egypt were long past. He now enjoyed the quiet life in the warmth and blue skies of the Sinai peninsula. He had memories enough for long years of reflection. For forty years he had lived in Egypt before his early and compulsory retirement began.

Indeed, he had led not one but two lives in those stormy decades. He was an Egyptian prince, raised in the palace of the Pharaoh, an adopted son of the royal family. Yet when servants attended him under the awning of a royal vessel on the Nile, he would remember again his mother's story of another vessel: a little basket made into a boat by a coating of tar. Moses was a Hebrew baby, born when the Pharaoh had decreed genocide for the Hebrew population of Egypt. All the male babies were to be put to death. The Hebrew women could then be absorbed, as servants and mistresses, into the Egyptian nation.

The "final solution" as practiced in Egypt had been less than effective. The God of Israel had given a baby boom to the enslaved Hebrews. Mothers found ways to hide their newborn children. Few, however, had found as effective a strategy as had been devised by Jochebed. She launched her little son in the Nile at the time and place where the princess of Egypt came to bathe. Miriam, Moses' sister, had been posted to watch. The princess did indeed discover the abandoned infant. She not only spared him; she adopted him and accepted Miriam's offer to find him a nurse—an action that was surely not naive on her part.

The strategy was wise, but Moses well knew why it was effective. The God of his fathers had touched the heart of the princess. Under the sentence of death, he had, like Joseph before him, been raised up to be a prince in Egypt.

How drastically the situation of Israel in Egypt had changed! In the years since Egypt had mourned the death of Joseph, Israel experienced rapid growth. The families of the twelve brothers swelled into a significant minority in the land of Egypt, a minority of foreigners who were viewed with suspicion by the Egyptians and by a Pharaoh who saw the Semites as a threat within his kingdom.

What calling did Moses have as a prince in Egypt? God had made Joseph a blessing to Egypt and Israel alike. But now the Egyptians were exploiting the people as slave labor. Their whips lashed out to exploit, to torture, and to abuse. Must Moses become in some way their deliverer? Yes, he must choose, choose between Egypt and Israel, between rule and slavery, between luxury and agony.

How vividly Moses remembered the day when he had struck out to defend his people! He had not followed any plan; he had not sought the counsel of the elders of the people. He had only stood by watching with growing anger a savage Egyptian taskmaster lashing the bloody back of a helpless Hebrew slave. There was no way to restrain the brute. His blood-lust served the policies of the Pharaoh. To stop him he would have to kill him. Moses looked about. No other Egyptians were in sight. The deed was quickly done, and as quickly Moses buried his victim in the sand.

Then came a great disillusionment. Did the word spread through the slave population that they had a champion in the court of the Pharaoh? Did Israel recognize that God had raised up a deliverer, a leader prepared to commit himself to their cause? The next day provided the answer. As he was again watching his people in their suffering, Moses saw two Hebrews fighting. Was it not enough that they should be beaten by the Egyptians? Must they also beat one another? Moses confronted the man who was in the wrong: "Why are you hitting your fellow Hebrew?"

His answer changed the life of Moses, instantly and utterly. "Who made you ruler and judge over us? Are you thinking of killing me as you killed the Egyptian?" (Ex. 2:13-14).

Moses saw that his deed was known. In the malice of that Israelite he saw not only the rejection of his leadership but the certainty of his betrayal. No Egyptian was witness to his stroke for liberation, but his own people were ready to use his deed against him. Soon enough the word was carried to Pharaoh, but Moses escaped to the wilderness of Sinai. There in his "retirement" he served as a shepherd, keeping the flocks of Jethro, who became his father-in-law.

It was, perhaps, no more than curiosity that caused Moses to notice a bush in the distance that was ablaze. That in itself was rather unusual, but more remarkable was the fact that when he looked again much later the bush was still burning. Moses hurried to investigate this remarkable spectacle.

God spoke to Moses from the fire of His glory, glory

that rested on the bush without burning it. With that address by the voice of the Lord there began a new era in God's plan of salvation. God had revealed himself to Jacob and Joseph by dreams and visions; he would reveal himself to Moses as directly as a man speaks with his friend. Yet the directness of God's address did not mean that there was no gulf to be bridged. Moses had to take the shoes from his feet; he stood on holy ground. The slopes of Mount Sinai had become the holiest spot on earth, for there the Lord Himself appeared in glory.

It is God who took the initiative. He called to Moses from the bush, declared that He had heard the groaning of Israel in captivity and that He remembered the promise He had made to the fathers. He identified Himself as the God of Abraham, Isaac, and Jacob. And He said that He had come down to deliver their descendants, to be their God and Savior.

The people could not deliver themselves. Their cause was hopeless; they were helpless in the power of the Egyptian empire. Further, the promises of God were such that only He could fulfill them. God promised more than the successful revolt of a slave population; He promised that they would be sent on their way out of Egypt heaped down with presents from the Egyptians. Without a single sword stroke (for they were without arms), they would carry out treasures from Egypt like the spoils of a conquering army. Further, they would be given the land of the promise, a land now inhabited by other nations, but a land that God had made their inheritance.

An even greater blessing was also promised. Israel was called out of Egypt to meet with God and to worship Him on the very mountain where Moses stood. God called Israel His people; Israel was His firstborn son. If the Pharaoh would not release God's firstborn, then God's judgment would fall on Pharaoh's firstborn and on the oldest son in every Egyptian household (Ex. 4:22-23). Beyond all that God would do for Israel lies what He would *be* to Israel: their God, the God of the covenant that He would establish with them at Sinai, as He had promised to the fathers.

Since the situation of Israel was so hopeless—and how well Moses knew that!—and since the promises of God were so great, God Himself had to come to keep His word. Moses did well to ask of God His name. Jacob long ago had asked for the name of the Angel of the Lord as the dawn ended their wrestling match. We might suppose that Moses requested God's name because many in Israel had forgotten the God of their fathers. Would they be in danger of confusing the God of Abraham with the gods of the Egyptians, with Ra or Amon or Osiris? Moses may well have recognized such a danger, but there was a deeper reason for his asking the name of the God whose glory shone from the bush.

Moses wanted to know by name the Lord who called him. He would seek for himself and for the people the privilege of addressing God by name. We rightly speak of names as "handles," for we lay hold of the person we call by name, especially by an intimate or personal name.

The name God gave to Moses is the name JAH. He is "I AM," the God whose existence is determined by Himself. We should not understand the name given to Moses in a philosophical sense. God was not announcing to Moses that He is pure Being. He was declaring His Lordship. He is the personal God, who may be addressed by name. He reveals Himself when and where He chooses. Later, when God again proclaimed His name to Moses, He said, "I will have mercy on whom I will have mercy" (Ex. 33:19). The "I Am" God determines His own purposes of mercy.

We may well reflect on the implications of God's wonderful name. His name, "I Am," affirms His existence as unique as well as personal. God does not define Himself as a member of a class of beings; He is not, for example, the sky god in contrast to an earth goddess. The pantheons of deities that men worship are set aside.

Yet much as we may learn from God's name, and much as we may dare to speculate about it, we are summoned by that name to hear the voice of the living God, to stand before Him who was, and is, and is coming. When Jesus declared, "I am," in the garden of Gethsemane, those who had come to arrest Him fell backward to the ground (Jn. 18:6). Every word of the Lord is filled with power. God speaks and it is done, He commands and it stands fast. But when God speaks His own name, the power of His word takes on a special significance.

An Israeli archaeologist tells of the thrill of recognizing the identity of a recently excavated text from ancient Israel. The inscription was in archaic characters, and the words were partly missing. But three times *Yahweh*, the name of the Lord, was repeated. The text was the blessing God gave to Aaron and to the priests to pronounce upon the people (English Bibles usually translate *Yahweh* as "LORD" in capital and small capital letters)[1]:

> The LORD bless you and keep you;
> the LORD make his face shine upon you
>   and be gracious to you;
> the LORD turn his face toward you
>   and give you peace. (Num. 6:24-26)

It was the first time the name of the Lord had been found on so ancient a text. Apparently it was a kind of medallion once worn by an ancient Israelite. When God gave the benediction the priests were to use, He said, "So they will put my name on the Israelites, and I will bless them" (Num. 6:27).

No doubt the power of God's name was at times debased into magic. Just as Israel once thought to compel God's blessing by carrying the ark into battle, so there were times when they used His name as a charm in amulets. But the power of God's name is not less than magic; it is infinitely more. The error of magic is to suppose that divine power can be manipulated by incantations or rituals. The truth of grace is that God binds Himself to His own name.

The living God is not the genie of Aladdin's lamp. It is He who summoned Moses, not Moses who summoned Him. Yet God named Himself as the God of Abraham, Isaac, and Jacob. He is the God of the promises; the very name that declares He is Lord declares that He is Lord of His chosen people. He calls them by name; better still, He calls them by *His* name (Is. 43:7). It is no accident that so many Old Testament names are compounded with -jah, -iah, or Jo- (Elijah, Adonijah, Jeremiah, Jonathan). These are all forms of God's holy name, borne by His people.

God called to Moses from the bush not only to announce His presence and His purpose but to commission Moses to act in His name. "So now, go. I am sending you to Pharaoh to bring my people the Israelites out of Egypt" (Ex. 3:10).

The delivering of Israel is God's work; He has heard their groaning and has come to save them. Nevertheless, God chose to save them through the ministry of Moses, His servant. On the one hand, Israel is the servant of the Lord. God demanded that Pharaoh release Israel, His son, "that he may serve me" (Ex. 4:23, KJV).[2] On the other hand, Moses is God's servant in a unique sense. He was called to be God's instrument in delivering Israel. To Moses, God would speak "face to face, clearly and not in riddles; he sees the form of the LORD" (Num. 12:8). Israel should fear to speak against "my servant Moses." To rebel against Moses is to reject the

Lord he serves.

The patriarchs were God's servants; they carried out a special role as the heads of their households. That role continued in the tribal chiefs, recognized as elders of the people. But God called Moses to be His servant in a new way. He held authority as a prophet, to bring God's word to the people; he was the ruler and judge of Israel; he led them through the wilderness, interceded with God for them when they sinned, and instructed them in the way. The figure of Moses was made the model for the prophets who were to follow.

More than that, in His calling of Moses, God established a pattern that pointed to the work of the Messiah: "I will raise up for them a prophet like you from among their brothers; I will put my words in his mouth, and he will tell them everything I command him" (Dt. 18:18).

Moses, the great servant over the house of God, prepares us for Isaiah's songs of the servant, and for the coming of God's Son as the final Servant, sent by the Father.

Moses was anything but eager to accept God's commission. He could picture the battle lines of Pharaoh's chariots; he could also hear the challenge of the brawling Israelite from forty years ago: "Who made you ruler and judge over us?" Moses now recognized his own limitations. He said, "Who am I, that I should go to Pharaoh and bring the Israelites out of Egypt?" (Ex. 3:11). Moses knew the might of Pharaoh and the weakness of Israel; he did not yet know the power of the Lord. Yet he believed God and went to Egypt. When he stood again at Mount Sinai, it was with the thousands upon thousands of the people of Israel.

God's great deliverance of Israel from the exploitation of their bondage was first of all a work of judgment. Joseph as the servant of the Lord had brought blessing to Egypt; Moses was given a sterner task. The miracles that God worked through Moses were plagues. God punished the Egyptians until they were glad to see Israel go. The sacred Nile was turned to blood; the land that worshiped the sun disk was plunged into total darkness. God showed by the plagues His power over all the idols of Egypt.

The drama of Israel's deliverance was played out between Moses as the spokesman of the Lord and Pharaoh as the adversary of the people of God. Moses did not lead a slave revolt; Israel even complained about his demands for their liberation, since the immediate result was to increase their Egyptian oppression. Liberation was not won by Israel; it was given by God, and Moses was God's spokesman.

This lesson was made unforgettable in the last act of the drama. Pharaoh repeatedly went back on his promise to release the people. When they had actually begun their march, he changed his mind again and sent his chariots storming after them. The war chariots of ancient Egypt were the great mobile striking force of their day, feared by the armies of the ancient world. They saw their quarry as a rabble of escaping slaves without arms and burdened with children, cattle, and cartloads of household goods. Escape was impossible, for the Egyptian army hemmed them in against the shores of the Red (or Reed) Sea.

The people again attacked Moses bitterly: "Was it because there were no graves in Egypt that you brought us to the desert to die? . . . Didn't we say to you in Egypt, 'Leave us alone; let us serve the Egyptians'? It would have been better for us to serve the Egyptians than to die in the desert!" (Ex. 14:11-12). Moses did not call for freedom fighters. Resistance was hopeless. He said, "Do not be afraid. Stand firm and you will see the deliverance the LORD will bring you today. The Egyptians you see today you will never see again. The LORD will fight for you; you need only to be still" (Ex. 14:13-14).

God Himself in the pillar of fire drove back the Egyptians and held them at bay for the night. In the morning God opened the sea so that Israel could pass over on dry ground. The Egyptians attempted to pursue and were destroyed by the returning waves. On the far side of the sea, Moses and Israel sang to Yahweh, "I will sing to the LORD, for he is highly exalted. The horse and its rider he has hurled into the sea. The LORD is my strength and my song; he has become my salvation" (Ex. 15:1-2).

This triumph song is repeated in the Psalms and in Isaiah to describe the future salvation of the people of God (Ps. 118:14; Is. 12:2). Quite evidently the whole narrative has the purpose of showing that Israel's great deliverance was God's work. "Salvation is of the LORD" is the great theme of the Bible, and God's royal saving power is nowhere portrayed more graphically than in God's great act in rescuing Israel from Egypt.

The exodus event is often appealed to by advocates of a "liberation theology." They wish to redefine the Christian doctrine of salvation to center on political liberation. They call Christians to take up arms against oppressive regimes in the name of Christ. (Usually the oppression they wish to resist is from right-wing rather than left-wing regimes.) They criticize the church for "spiritualizing" the exodus, making it an analogy for salvation from sin rather than an instance of social and political liberation.

To be sure, Israel was delivered from slavery and political oppression. God did hear the groanings of His people under the lash. Yet Israel was not delivered through guerilla warfare. It was God's miraculous intervention that judged Egypt and set Israel free. The plight of the people of Israel could be described in political as well as spiritual terms, but the means of their deliverance was God's power and grace.

The way in which God freed Israel points to His purpose in doing so. God is indeed their Liberator: "I am the LORD your God, who brought you out of Egypt so that you would no longer be slaves to the Egyptians; I broke the bars of your yoke and enabled you to walk with heads held high" (Lev. 26:13).

God's purpose, however, was not simply to deliver Israel from Pharaoh's yoke. It was to bring them under His yoke. God demanded that Pharaoh let the people go that they might serve Him. When the people reached Mount Sinai and camped there, God had this message for them: "You yourselves have seen what I did to Egypt, and how I carried you on eagles' wings and brought you to myself. Now if you obey me fully and keep my covenant, then out of all nations you will be my treasured possession. Although the whole earth is mine, you will be for me a kingdom of priests and a holy nation" (Ex. 19:4-6).

The Lord brought Israel out of Egypt that He might gather them at His feet. They were borne on eagles' wings to God's own presence that He might claim them as His holy people, the treasure of His grace.

The Passover powerfully symbolized God's claim on Israel. Because Pharaoh would not free God's firstborn son, Israel, God in judgment claimed the firstborn son in the house of Pharaoh, and in every other family of Egypt. We might suppose that this judgment would pose no threat to Israel. (In the earlier plagues, Israel in the land of Goshen was spared.) But we learn that the angel of death was sent to bring judgment on every Israelite home as well. In the ceremonial law later given to Israel, the firstfruit of the harvest and the firstborn of the stock was viewed as representative of all the rest. God put His claim upon it to signify that all belonged to Him.

The life of the firstborn son was forfeit for two very different reasons: first, that God could claim every creature as His own; second, that sinful creatures stand under the judgment of God. The infliction of that judgment on the firstborn would represent the penalty due to all. If God in His righteousness were to exact this penalty of the sinful Egyptians, Israel could not escape and be spared. All have sinned and come short of the glory of God, Israel as well as Egypt.

God's provision of the Passover lamb clearly shows that the demand of God's justice must be met if His mercy is to be shown. A lamb without blemish was chosen by every Israelite household. The lamb was killed, and its blood put on the lintel and doorposts of the house. The angel of death, seeing the blood, passed over that household. The blood showed that death had taken place. The lamb had died in the place of the oldest son, and therefore also in the place of the others represented by the oldest son. Israel, in the symbolism of the Passover, was freed not just from the burden of bondage but from the guilt of sin. Their eating of the lamb, like their eating of the peace offerings, marked the restored fellowship with God that comes through the atonement God provides. They were to eat the Passover in their traveling clothes because God's promise is sure.

The Passover lamb provided an image of the work of salvation that God would perform. The event of the exodus from Egypt was similarly revealing, blending ceremonial and historical symbolism. God foreshadows by His deeds as well as His words what it meant for Him to claim sinners as His precious possession.

Jesus Christ fulfilled the ceremonial law. He is the Lamb of God who takes away the sin of the world. He is our Passover, sacrificed for us. Our meal of fellowship with God is His communion feast. Not only do these symbols point to Christ. The whole story points to Christ.

It is significant that on the Mount of Transfiguration,

Moses and Elijah talked with Jesus about the "exodus" He had to accomplish at Jerusalem. He who was offered as the sacrificial lamb was also the Savior and Liberator. He came to proclaim liberty to the captive, and He broke the ultimate yoke of bondage to liberate *all* the people of God.

God Establishes His Covenant

If God exists, why doesn't He prove it? Why doesn't God appear with lightning and thunder to accompany His presence? The story of the Bible gives a full answer to this question. God did so appear; He will appear again. The reason He does not now appear is not that He is reluctant to persuade atheists but the opposite.

God withholds the burning revelation of His holy presence because He withholds the day of judgment that it must bring. The God of glory has already revealed Himself as the Father of mercy by sending His Son into the world. He restrains the glory of His appearing so that men may respond to the call of His mercy and taste the wonder of His love. Men who demand that God show Himself do not know what they are asking! "Who can endure the day of his coming? Who can stand when he appears?" (Mal. 3:2).

God did appear in glory at Mount Sinai. The people were led by Moses to the very place where God had spoken from the flaming bush. But this time not just a bush but the whole mountain was in flames. The earth shook, rocks broke open. But most dreadful of all was a sound more awesome than the crashing thunder: the sound of the voice of the living God.

The author of Hebrews describes the terror of that scene: the mountain burning with fire, the darkness, gloom, and storm (Heb. 12:18-21). Then the heavenly trumpets sounded and God spoke. The people who heard those words begged that they might never again be exposed to such terror.

They asked Moses to intervene for them. Let *him* ascend that fearful mountain and hear the voice of God!

Note the way in which the author of Hebrews speaks of that event. We have not come to Mount Sinai. We do not approach what he calls a "palpable fire." We do not hear the trumpets and the voice of God. Does the author of Hebrews imply, then, that all such intrusions of heavenly glory are now over and done with? Does he counsel us about living in a secular world where God's presence is no longer evident and where there is nothing to be afraid of anymore?

By no means. Sinai is a mountain on this earth. The fire on Sinai, awesome as it was, was yet a physical fire, a fire that could be touched. When we gather for worship, the inspired writer tells us, we do not come to Mount Sinai but to Mount Zion. We gather before God not at the mountain in the wilderness, the trysting place where God met with His redeemed people; we gather instead at the goal of their pilgrimage, at Zion, the mountain of God's dwelling, the place where His glory abides.

Indeed, the mountain to which we come is not the earthly Mount Zion. It is the heavenly Zion, the Jerusalem that is above. In Christian worship we assemble with all God's holy ones, the myriads upon myriads of the holy angels and the spirits of just men made perfect. Our approach in worship is not to an earthly sanctuary, for we enter God's presence with Jesus Christ, our heavenly High Priest. The blood of Christ, sprinkled on the very throne of God is the assurance of our pardon. Our worship is not less supernatural than the experience of Israel in the wilderness. It is infinitely more so. We have emerged from the shadows into the reality.

The fire on Mount Sinai was merely touchable, but the fire to which we come is the flame of God's own presence. "Our 'God is a consuming fire'" (Heb. 12:29). We hear

God's voice, too, in a more immediate way, for God has spoken to us in His own Son. "See to it that you do not refuse him who speaks. If they did not escape when they refused him who warned them on earth, how much less will we, if we turn away from him who warns us from heaven?" (Heb. 12:25).

When Jesus, praying on a mountaintop, was transfigured in the presence of Peter, James, and John, they saw Moses and Elijah with Him. Moses had heard the voice of God on the top of Sinai; later, Elijah had been brought to that same mountain to hear God speak, not in the fire and the tempest, but in the quiet whisper of God's sovereign word. The cloud of glory that had surrounded Moses on Sinai again enveloped Jesus and His disciples. God's voice again spoke from the cloud. But God did not proclaim another ten commandments to be added to the words of His covenant of old. Rather, the voice from the cloud said, "This is my Son, whom I have chosen; listen to him" (Lk. 9:35).

God spoke from Sinai, called Abraham, revealed Himself to Jacob in dreams, and addressed Israel through the prophets—"but in these last days he has spoken to us by his Son, whom he appointed heir of all things, and through whom he made the universe" (Heb. 1:2).

In the marvel of the Incarnation, Jesus Christ has spoken to us the words that were given Him from the Father. Jesus is God's last Word. The words that He speaks to us are spirit and life. Israel could not bear to hear the voice of God. Moses, God's prophet, received God's words and spoke them to the people. Moses was the great servant in the house of God, but Jesus is the Son over the house.

Sinai was indeed a mountaintop in God's revelation. Those who quarrel about the authority of Scripture and question whether God's truth can be expressed in human language need to stand with Israel at the foot of Sinai and

hear the voice of God. Yet God had planned a greater revelation for which Sinai was still preparation: His revelation in
Jesus Christ. God's word to us is, "Hear Him!"

The author of Hebrews who describes for us the heavenly assembly that we enter in our worship also tells us not to
forsake the assembling of ourselves together on earth (Heb.
10:25). The church of Christ is His assembly. Indeed, that is
the meaning of the New Testament word for church: *ecclesia*.
Jesus used the word for "assembly" when He replied to the
confession of Simon Peter. Jesus said, "On this rock I will
build my church" (Mt. 16:18). His term would have been
well understood by the disciples, for Israel was God's
assembly.

Three times a year Israel was to assemble before the
Lord in Jerusalem to celebrate His feasts. Those assemblies
recalled the great assembly at Mount Sinai when the Lord
gathered His people before Him and established His covenant with them. Israel was a "congregation" because they
were brought into the assembly of God's holy ones. Moses,
in his blessing of the people before his death, painted a
spectacular picture of the meaning of the assembly at Sinai
(Dt. 33:1-5). There was God, enthroned as King in the midst
of the ten thousands of His holy angels. Israel was gathered at
His feet to receive His words. This Old Testament picture
was vivid in the thoughts of the Qumran Covenanters whose
scrolls were discovered in caves on the western shore of the
Dead Sea. This sect recognized that to join the congregation
of God was to enter into the assembly where the earthly holy
ones joined the heavenly angels.[3]

As the Mediator of the New Covenant, Jesus gathers
together the lost and scattered people of God. His calling
fulfills the festival assemblies of the ceremonial law. He calls
His people to His table, for He is the true Passover. He sends
His Spirit upon His assembled disciples at the feast of Pente-

cost. One great feast remains: the feast of Tabernacles, the great harvest-home feast for all the redeemed. In the heavenly Jerusalem, the author of Hebrews tells us, that festival assembly has already gathered. To that feast we call the nations of the earth. In the Great Commission Jesus sends us to gather with Him. He is lifted up that He might draw all men to Himself.

In the great assembly at Sinai God spoke to His people. He gave them His law in the context of His redemption. The Ten Commandments begin with God's description of Himself as the Redeemer of Israel: "I am the LORD your God, who brought you out of Egypt, out of the land of slavery" (Ex. 20:2).

The great mistake of legalism is to detach the law of God from the God who gave it. The Ten Commandments are not an abstract code of duty hung in the void. The first commandment governs the rest: "You shall have no other gods before me." God's people stand in His presence. He is their God; they are His people. Assembled there before Him, they must acknowledge Him as God alone. They are to love Him with all their heart, soul, strength, and mind.

The Lord is a jealous God (Ex. 20:4-5). He will not consent to be worshiped as one of a pantheon of deities. The jealousy of God is not like the envious and spiteful passion that we often describe with the word. The term that we translate "jealous" could also be translated "zealous." It refers to the intense and exclusive love God has for His people, a love that is to be requited by the pure devotion of Israel.

All the commandments of God's covenant focus on the heart of the covenant relation, the bond between God and His people. We have already seen that the Lord instituted marriage in the creation of Adam and Eve, and that He revealed in that ordinance the mysterious intensity of an exclusive love. The seventh commandment, therefore, has its setting in God's covenant with Israel. The jealous love of marital devotion is given by God Himself as a pattern of the love of His covenant. Marital faithfulness would, of course, strengthen family life in Israel when God's commandment was obeyed. Yet that command always pointed beyond itself to the faithful love of God for His people, and His call for their jealous devotion in return.

The command "You shall not commit adultery" applies to the most intimate of human relations, the demand of love that has its source in God, the God of the covenant. It is no mere metaphor when Hosea and Ezekiel cry out against the spiritual adultery of idol worship. Paul shows the priority of God's love in Jesus Christ when he addresses Christian wives and husbands (Eph. 5:22-33). He is not confusing the figure with the reality; he is pointing us to the love of God from which all true human love must spring.

We cannot understand the Ten Commandments apart from Jesus Christ. If we view them only as a list of "don'ts" from which we may infer a corresponding list of "dos," we forget the Lord who spoke the words from Sinai and the context in which He spoke them. God's commandments call His people to acknowledge Him as their Savior and Lord.

Israel, however, did not keep God's commandments. Paul can point out in Romans that all have sinned: not only the Gentiles whom God abandoned to their own rebellion, but also Israel, who had the law and did not keep it. The law therefore condemns the sin of those who break it. In that negative way the law points us to Christ. It shows what God's righteousness requires, and therefore shows us that we cannot satisfy God's just demands. We need Christ to save us from the curse of the law by bearing its penalty for us (Gal. 3:10-14).

Christ does not just bear the punishment that we

deserve. He also keeps the law in our place. Christ, our sin-bearer, gives to us the perfect robe of His righteousness. "God made him who had no sin to be sin for us, so that in him we might become the righteousness of God" (2 Cor. 5:21). The salvation that is ours in Christ is not just a restoration to innocence, with the debt of sin cancelled. Far less is it a second chance to earn our own salvation by having our slate wiped clean. What we receive in Christ is His righteousness; we are adopted into the perfect sonship of the second Adam and the true Israel (Ro. 9:5; 10:4; 1 Cor. 15:22,45).

To begin with, the law at Sinai expresses God's demand for perfect obedience. God is perfectly holy, and can require nothing less. In that respect His law can only condemn us. But God did not bring His people out of Egypt to consume them in the flame of Sinai. His purpose was to save them. There is, therefore, another aspect to the law that God gave. It is the law of God's covenant with His redeemed people. The people entered into covenant with God. They promised to keep all the words that God spoke (Ex. 24:3). Sacrifices were offered, and both the altar and the people were sprinkled with the blood of the sacrifice. From the very outset, therefore, it was clear that atonement must be made, and that the atonement must come from God's altar.

Christ's coming is not a divine afterthought. The blood of the covenant sprinkled at Sinai witnesses to the sacrifice of the Lamb of God chosen from the foundation of the world. We may distinguish between the Ten Commandments and the ceremonial law, but we need to remember that they were given together. God did not speak words that could only condemn His people without providing the symbols of atonement.

Since this is so, we may understand that even the content of the Ten Commandments may point us to Jesus

Christ. God's jealousy for His own righteousness is also jealousy for His plan of salvation. Consider the second commandment. Why did God forbid the making of images for worship? We have already seen that it was not because an image is impossible, for God made man in His image. Why, then, did God prohibit man from worshiping Him through images? The answer is that God was jealous for His coming revelation through Jesus Christ. No image or likeness was to be placed between the cherubim on the "mercy-seat" because God in His own time would send His incarnate Son, at whose feet the perfume of Mary's devotion could rightly be poured. Jesus Christ is the image of the invisible God. In His human nature, He reveals the Father: "Anyone who has seen me has seen the Father" (Jn. 14:9). Worship apart from images means worship apart from any image *except* the one God has sent: His only-begotten Son.

The third commandment expresses God's zeal for His holy name. God shows the depth of that zeal in His jealousy for the name of Jesus, the only name under heaven given among men by which we must be saved. God exalts the name of Jesus above every name, that at the name of Jesus every knee should bow and every tongue confess that Jesus Christ is Lord. If Jesus were not God's eternal Son, such worship would be sacrilege. But God sets apart His own name, making it holy and glorious, as He lifts up the name of Jesus.

So, too, the Sabbath commandment is made for man, but especially for the Son of Man, who is the Lord of the Sabbath and transforms it into the Lord's Day by His Resurrection. The rest that the Sabbath represents is the final rest that Christ provides (Heb. 4:9-11).

When we hear God's law given from Sinai, therefore, we must not only tremble at its thunder and flee to Christ for His forgiveness and righteousness. We must also hear in it God's zeal for His own Son, and find in it witness to the redemptive purpose of the God who redeemed Israel from the house of bondage.

Jesus kept the law for us; He learned obedience through the things He suffered. In His obedience, He was not only our representative, but our example. He transformed and deepened the law even as he fulfilled it. He enables us to understand the will of our heavenly Father as we understand the covenant made at Sinai. Above all, He renews us by His Spirit so that we may do what the law asks: love the Lord our God with all our heart, soul, strength, and mind, and our neighbor as ourself.

NOTES:
1. Because the name *Yahweh* was regarded as too holy to pronounce, it was read as "Lord" in the synagogue. In the Masoretic text of the Old Testament, the vowels of the word for "Lord" (*Adonai*) were written into the consonants of Yahweh (Y or J, H, W or V, and H), yielding a composite that the ASV transliterated as "Jehovah." Ancient Hebrew was written without vowels. "Yahweh" is a probable but not certain form of the name. The New Testament, following the Greek version of the Old Testament, uses "Lord" (*Kurios*) for Yahweh.
2. The NIV translates "so he may worship me." The thought of worship may indeed be foremost here, but the term describes the service that Israel brings to the Lord. Israel is delivered from serving Pharaoh to serving God.
3. "God has given them [heavenly blessings] to His chosen ones as an everlasting possession, and has caused them to inherit the lot of the Holy Ones. He has joined their assembly to the Sons of heaven . . ." (1QS 11:7-8—G. Vermes, *The Dead Sea Scrolls in English* [Baltimore: Penguin Books, 1962], page 93). See also Carol Newsom, *Songs of the Sabbath Sacrifice* (Atlanta: Scholars Press, 1985). Our English word "saints" applies only to human beings; in both Hebrew and Greek the term for "holy ones" may refer to angels as well.

6
THE ROCK OF MOSES:
IS THE LORD AMONG US?

At Sinai God gave Israel not only the law of His covenant, but also the tent of His dwelling. God would be their God by His presence as well as by His word. In the cloud on Mount Sinai, Moses received detailed instructions for the building of the tabernacle, the tent that would be the house of God in the midst of the tents of Israel.

For forty days Moses remained on top of the mountain, screened from Israel by the cloud of God's presence. When he at last began his descent, he held in his hands the tablets of stone on which God had written the words of His law. Yet the weight of God's law in his hands was less than a weight he carried on his heart. God had given Moses a final command: to go down to a people who had already turned away from the covenant they had so solemnly affirmed. Moses carried the command God had thundered from Sinai: "You shall not make for yourself an idol. . . ." But God told Moses that the people down below had already made an idol in the form of a golden calf. They had worshiped it and sacrificed to it.

Moses' foreboding was heightened as he heard the sounds coming from the camp below. Joshua, who was attending Moses, thought that he heard the sound of battle. Moses replied, "It is not the sound of victory, it is not the sound of defeat; it is the sound of singing that I hear" (Ex. 32:18).

When Moses could see as well as hear the licentious orgy at the foot of the mountain, it was too much for him. In anger he flung down the tablets of God's law; they shattered at his feet. Then God's judgment broke up the riot of rebellious idolatry. Moses stood at the entrance of the camp and called out for those who were for the Lord. Only the Levites, Moses' own tribe, rallied to him. Moses commissioned them to execute God's sentence on the rebels. About three thousand died as the Levites carried out their grim task.

Moses returned to meet with the Lord. What future could there be for Israel? If the people completely violated God's covenant at the very foot of the mountain where God was still speaking, what point was there in continuing the covenant relation? Was not Israel already judged and rejected? Moses pled with God not to blot Israel out of the book of life, but to blot out his name instead. The apostle Paul, centuries later, reflected that plea of Moses. Paul, too, servant of the Lord in the New Covenant, said that he would be willing to be cursed and cut off from Christ "for the sake of my brothers, those of my own race, the people of Israel" (Ro. 9:3-4).

The Lord would not remove the name of Moses from His book. Instead, He proposed to Moses an alternative plan for the relation of God to Israel. God would not dwell in the midst of Israel. That was too dangerous, for they were a "stiff-necked" people, proud and rebellious. If God were to go up in the midst of them even for a moment, His presence could destroy them (Ex. 33:5).

God's alternate plan did not default on His promises. He would go before the people in the presence of His angel. He would lead them into the land of promise, defeat their enemies, drive out the wicked inhabitants of the land, and give them their promised possession. But He would not go up in their midst.

There would then be no need to build the tabernacle, for the purpose of that construction was to provide a tent in which God could dwell in the midst of the people of Israel; His tent was to be in the center of the camp, their tents pitched around it, according to their tribes. Rather than setting up the tabernacle, Moses would continue the practice that had apparently been begun already. He would have a "tent of meeting" set up well outside the camp. God would come to the door of that tent in the cloud of glory to meet with Moses. When Moses went out to the tent, the people would stand respectfully to watch him go. When the cloud descended they were to worship. If any man needed to inquire of the Lord, he could go out to the tent and speak with Moses.

The change that God proposed was not in substituting an angel for His own presence. The Angel of the Lord was theophanous, the appearing of God in the form of His messenger. "Do not rebel against him; he will not forgive your rebellion, since my Name is in him" (Ex. 23:21). The issue was rather whether the Lord would go before the people in the presence of His Angel, drive out their enemies, and give them the land, or whether God would go up in the midst of them. Should the tabernacle be built so that God could be in their midst, or should God continue to come to the door of the tent of meeting, at a distance from the camp?

We might suppose that Moses would have welcomed God's proposal. Surely the danger of God's holy presence in the midst of the camp of Israel was obvious. What advantages would Israel lose under the new arrangement? They still had access to God. They still had Moses as their mediator. They still had God leading them through the desert and the guarantee of His gift of the land.

Indeed, what God proposed seems to be precisely what many people today want of religion. They do not want to lose all contact with God, but prefer that their relations with Him be handled by a professional. Let a clergyman do the praying. It is well to have God available at no great distance. We might need His help—in a counseling center perhaps, or as a national deity who could restrain the Kremlin. But to have God at the center of our lives—that is decidedly too close. His presence would be most inconvenient for some of our business deals, our entertainment, or our grabbing a little of the gusto that the TV commercials advertise.

Knowing Israel as he did, did Moses at once close on God's offer, thanking Him for His thoughtfulness in deciding to be God at a convenient distance? Quite to the contrary. Moses was distraught, and went into profound mourning. Following his lead, Israel mourned, too. They put off their jewelry (the gold that had not been melted down for the golden calf), and waited while Moses went to speak with God. Again Moses poured out his heart before the Lord. Had not God said that he knew Moses by name? Was not Israel God's people? "If your Presence does not go with us, do not send us up from here. How will anyone know that you are pleased with me and with your people unless you go with us? What else will distinguish me and your people from all the other people on the face of the earth?" (Ex. 33:15-16).

Nothing could compare with the immediate presence of God in the midst of His people. The favor for which Moses prayed was obviously not based on the performance record of Israel. He was pleading for the favor of grace, the favor of

God's calling that had distinguished His people from all the other nations. If God were not to seal that favor with His own presence, the whole enterprise was useless. Why go to the land of promise in any case? Moses sought the land, not because the milk and honey of Canaan was to be preferred to the fish and lentils of Egypt, but because the land of Israel was the place where God would set His name, the place of His house among His people. If God were not to dwell among His people, there would be no point in going to the place of His choosing.

God's covenant was that He would be their God, and they His people; fellowship with God was the heart of the covenant. To seal his request, Moses sought exactly what God's presence in the midst offered: the revelation of God's glory. "Now show me your glory," prayed Moses (Ex. 33:18).

Was this a strange request? Had not Moses seen the glory of the Lord in the cloud? Had he not communed with God as he received His commandments? Yes, but Moses yearned for a fuller knowledge of the Lord. God had said that He knew Moses by name; Moses likewise wanted to know God by name in a full and personal encounter.

Moses could not plead for the continuance of God's presence on the basis of what Israel had done or would do. He could not offer to God the kind of excuses about the golden calf that Aaron had offered to him. If he would secure God's continuing presence, his only appeal had to be to the nature of God Himself, to the covenant faithfulness of the God of grace. To secure God's favor, Moses asked Him to reveal Himself, to proclaim His name.

This is what God did. He could not permit Moses to see the full glory of His face, but He would allow him to see His back. God covered Moses in the crevice of a rock while His glory passed by. He proclaimed His name afresh to Moses:

the "I AM" God, who would be gracious to whom He would be gracious. His sovereign mercy was the hope of Moses and of Israel. He is eternally the God who is "full of grace and truth."

Moses' prayer was answered. God would go with His people. The tabernacle would be built to symbolize His presence in the midst. The plan of the tabernacle presents a double image: on the one hand, there were barriers that cordoned off God's holiness; on the other, a way of access was opened by His grace. The curtains of the tabernacle screened off the glory of the Lord's presence, but a way of approach was provided.

The worshiper could enter the courtyard and offer his sacrifice at the great bronze altar in the forecourt. The priests, after washing at the laver, could enter the holy place to pray to God at the altar of burnt incense. Beyond the holy place was the holy of holies, where the ark of the covenant was kept. Into that sanctuary only the high priest could go, and then only once a year on the day of atonement. Nevertheless, the tabernacle provided the open way into the presence of the Lord who dwelt in the midst of His people.

His request granted, Moses prayed one of the most beautiful prayers in the Bible: "If now I have found grace in thy sight, O Lord, let my Lord, I pray thee, go among us; for it is a stiff-necked people, and pardon our iniquity and our sin, and take us for thine inheritance" (Ex. 34:9, KJV).

Because the people of Israel were stiff-necked, God had said that He could not go in their midst. But for that very reason, Moses asked God to go with them, forgiving their iniquity and sin. He does not ask God to give Israel their inheritance, but to take Israel as His inheritance. Moses laid hold of God's grace, and prayed that God would make Israel His prized possession.

John holds this passage in view in the first chapter of his

Gospel (Jn. 1:14-18). He reminds us that the law was given by Moses, but that the "grace and truth" of which Moses wrote (Ex. 34:6) came through Jesus Christ. Throughout the Gospel of John, we learn of the way in which Moses testified of Christ. Jesus said, "If you believed Moses, you would believe me, for he wrote about me" (Jn. 5:46).

When John says "No man hath seen God at any time; the only begotten Son, which is in the bosom of the Father, he hath declared him" (Jn. 1:18, KJV), he is thinking of God's revelation to Moses. Moses had not been permitted to see God, but the full glory of God has now been revealed in Jesus Christ.

Some Bible translations lose the force of John's testimony by not translating literally John's word for "tenting" or "tabernacling": "And the Word became flesh, and tabernacled among us (and we beheld his glory, glory as of the only begotten from the Father), full of grace and truth" (Jn. 1:14, ASV margin).

Here John is declaring the fulfillment of the revelation of God to Moses. The issue was God's presence in the midst of His people. The symbol of that continuing presence was the tabernacle; there the glory of the God who is "full of grace and truth" was revealed. But what was a symbol in the time of Moses has become a reality in Jesus Christ. The true and abiding Tabernacle is not a tent of goat skins, but the incarnate Lord. Even the glory cloud is but a symbol of the presence of the Lord; Jesus is the Lord Himself, the true Temple.

Jesus could tell the woman of Samaria that not even Jerusalem was the place where God must be worshiped, because the hour had come when He must be worshiped in Spirit and in truth: in Spirit, because Jesus could give her the water of the Spirit; in truth, because Jesus was the Truth, the reality of which the Temple was the symbol. That hour was coming with Jesus' death and resurrection; indeed, that hour had already come because Jesus had already come: "I who speak to you am he" (Jn. 4:26).

Both the tablets of the law and the tabernacle were given by God at Sinai. Both point to Christ, who is the fulfillment of the law to all who believe and who is the heavenly Priest, the Lamb of God, and the true Tabernacle. Both the law and the worship at Sinai were expressions of God's covenant, a covenant fulfilled in Jesus Christ in whom it was made new. It was not just in the institutions of the covenant that Christ was anticipated, however. He was also foreshadowed in the history of the covenant. The story of redemption in the Old Testament is the story of Jesus.

God led Israel on from Sinai as they journeyed toward Canaan. His purpose in leading them was not rapid transportation. It was education. Moses reflected on God's curriculum as the covenant was renewed with a second generation at the border of Canaan:

> "Remember how the LORD your God led you all the way in the desert these forty years, to humble you and to test you in order to know what was in your heart, whether or not you would keep his commands. He humbled you, causing you to hunger and then feeding you with manna, which neither you nor your fathers had known, to teach you that man does not live on bread alone but on every word that comes from the mouth of the LORD. . . . Know then in your heart that as a man disciplines his son, so the LORD your God disciplines you." (Dt. 8:2-5)

The word of the Lord by which Israel was to live was not only the word spoken from Sinai. It was also the word that directed Israel's journeys day by day. The people were humbled, tested, taught that God was faithful, and shown His unfailing provision. God showed Israel their own helplessness in order that they might find Him to be their help in every distress. His instruction went beyond testing. By His deeds of deliverance He also pictured the spiritual reality of the covenant. God's feeding them with manna, for example, graphically portrayed the truth that life is God's gift and that His children are given the bread of heaven from their Father.

Jesus pointed this out to the crowds He fed in the wilderness. He fed more than five thousand from the five loaves and two fish in a boy's lunch basket. But for many the miracle was not spectacular enough. They demanded a more astonishing provision of bread. Let Jesus give manna in the desert as Moses had done. Jesus answered in a way that showed that the manna was a type of God's spiritual provision: "I tell you the truth, it is not Moses who has given you the bread from heaven, but it is my Father who gives you the true bread from heaven. For the bread of God is he who comes down from heaven and gives life to the world" (Jn. 6:32-33).

As the words of Jesus show, there is more that a superficial allegory to be found in God's giving of the manna. The Lord's provision of life from above points beyond physical nourishment. If food were the only thing missing for the people, they need not have left Egypt. Indeed, many of them preferred the leeks and fish of Egypt to the manna: "We detest this miserable food!" (Num. 21:5). God gave the manna to teach about His gift of spiritual life through faith. Israel was taught to trust God for daily bread in more than a physical sense. Thus there was good reason for a pot of manna to be placed within the ark of the covenant.

The instructional content of the wilderness episodes pointed forward as well as upward. Israel was taught to anticipate the future blessings promised in God's covenant.

For example, when the bitter water of Marah was healed at God's command, God made the incident a sign of His covenant promise: "I am the LORD, who heals you" (Ex. 15:26). The tree that Moses cast into the bitter water became a sign of God's removal of the curse by the sweetness and balm of the tree of life (Gen. 2:9; Ezk. 47:12).[1]

Through the history of God's dealings with His covenant people, this promise was repeated. Jeremiah cried, "Is there no balm in Gilead? Is there no physician there?" (Jer. 8:22). He prayed, "Heal me, O LORD, and I will be healed; save me and I will be saved, for you are the one I praise" (Jer. 17:14).

In answer, God repeated His promise to His prophet and His people: "But I will restore you to health and heal your wounds" (Jer. 30:17; 33:6). God Himself would come to remove the curse and to heal and restore His people: "'He will come to save you.' Then will the eyes of the blind be opened and the ears of the deaf unstopped. Then will the lame leap like a deer, and the tongue of the dumb shout for joy" (Is. 35:4-6).

God Himself promised to be the Healer of His people; yet His healing work was to be accomplished through His Anointed. This Messiah would bind up the brokenhearted and comfort those who mourn, for He would bring in the year of God's favor (Is. 61:1-2). In Isaiah's amazing description of the Suffering Servant of the Lord, we learn that He would come to bear our griefs and sicknesses, and that by His wounds we are healed (Is. 53:5). Matthew describes the healing ministry of Jesus on a Sabbath evening in Capernaum, and then reminds us of these words: "He took up our infirmities and carried our diseases" (Mt. 8:17; cf. Is. 53:4). God's sign of healing at Marah and all His care for Israel in the wilderness was preparation on the screen of history for the fulfillment that was yet to come with Jesus Christ.

This is clear in another remarkable incident in the desert. When a second generation of wandering Israelites rebelled against God's direction of their march, God judged their revolt by sending poisonous serpents among them. They cried for deliverance, and God commanded Moses to forge a serpent of brass and lift it up on the standard (perhaps the rod of the Lord). The people were commanded to look at the serpent of brass, and those who looked were healed and lived (Num. 21:4-9).

Jesus referred to this event when He described His mission to Nicodemus, a member of the Sanhedrin who came to him by night. "Just as Moses lifted up the snake in the desert, so the Son of Man must be lifted up, that everyone who believes may have eternal life in him" (Jn. 3:14-15, NIV margin). The brass serpent, the image of the curse upon Israel, was lifted up as a sign of God's power over the curse and His deliverance from it.

Jesus must have amazed Nicodemus by comparing the "lifting up" of the Son of Man to the lifting up of the serpent. The Son of Man was the glorious figure described in Daniel's prophecy (Dan. 7:13-14). Daniel depicted Him as coming on the clouds of heaven to receive the rule of God's eternal Kingdom. How could such a glorious figure be compared to the metal effigy of a poisonous snake?

The comparison is profound. Jesus is the Son of Man; He spoke of His being lifted up to glory as beginning with His being lifted up to the cross. When He said, "But I, when I am lifted up from the earth, will draw all men to myself" (Jn. 12:32), He was referring not merely to His ascension but to "the kind of death he was going to die" (Jn. 12:33).

Jesus was "lifted up" and exposed on the cross as one accursed. That in itself was enough to convince Saul the Pharisee that Jesus could not be the Messiah. Jesus had been crucified, and the law of God said that anyone hung on a tree was cursed (Dt. 21:23). But after Christ appeared to Saul on the road to Damascus, he came to understand that the very event that seemed to disprove the Messiahship of Jesus was its demonstration. Saul the persecutor became Paul the apostle, resolved to know nothing but Christ and Him crucified. He taught that "Christ redeemed us from the curse of the law by becoming a curse for us, for it is written: 'Cursed is everyone who is hung on a tree'" (Gal. 3:13).

Like the serpent on the rod, Christ on the cross was the embodiment of the curse. He bore the judgment of death because He bore the guilt of sin. He was smitten of God and afflicted because the Lord laid on Him the iniquity of us all (Is. 53:6). "God made him who had no sin to be sin for us, so that in him we might become the righteousness of God" (2 Cor. 5:21). At the cross God triumphed over the powers of darkness; the lifting up of Christ on the cross was followed by the resurrection and His being lifted up to glory (Jn. 13:31; Acts 5:31). Jesus also had His ascension to glory in view: "No one has ever gone into heaven except the one who came from heaven—the Son of Man, who is in heaven" (Jn. 3:13, NIV margin).

As we saw in connection with Jacob's dream, Jesus Himself was the ultimate answer to the question of Agur in the book of Proverbs (30:4): "Who has gone up to heaven and come down? Who has gathered up the wind in the hollow of his hands? . . . What is his name, and the name of his son? Tell me if you know!"

Jesus, who came down from heaven, ascended to heaven: his "lifting up" began at the cross. God triumphed over the curse in the victory of Calvary (Col. 2:13-15).

From early in the wilderness wanderings of Israel comes the most vivid image of the triumph of God's grace in His covenant with Israel. Only a few months after the deliverance of Israel from Egypt, the Lord brought them to Rephidim on the way to Mount Sinai (Ex. 17:1-7). There was no water where they camped. In the arid climate of the Sinai desert, dehydration takes place in hours rather than days. When their waterskins became empty, death was certain. "So they quarreled with Moses and said, 'Give us water to drink.'"

Unfortunately, the word "quarrel" does not adequately express the meaning of the Hebrew term. "They lodged a complaint with Moses" would be closer to the meaning. The word is the root of "Meribah," the name given to the place of this incident (Ex. 17:7).[2] It is a legal term describing the institution of a lawsuit. In the prophets it is used to express the lawsuit that God brought against Israel because they broke His covenant (Mic. 6:1-8). Meribah designated Israel's lawsuit against God.

The legal action the people proposed to take was first against Moses. "Why did you bring us up out of Egypt to make us and our children and livestock die of thirst?" Moses, they charged, was guilty of treason and deserved to be executed by stoning. They would stone Moses, not as an act of mob violence, but as the execution of the death sentence by the community. If their bones were to bleach under the fierce sun, then let Moses first pay the penalty.

Understandably, Moses protested: "Why do you [bring charges against] me? Why do you put the LORD to the test?" It is not really Moses but *God* that the people would put on trial: "Is the LORD among us or not?" (Ex. 17:7).

God had brought Israel into the desert to make His covenant with them. He led them in order to teach them; testing was part of the training process. At the end of the journey, Moses would eventually to say to them:

> "Remember how the LORD your God led you all the
> way in the desert these forty years, to humble you and

to test you in order to know what was in your heart, whether or not you would keep his commands. He humbled you, causing you to hunger and then feeding you with manna, which neither you nor your fathers had known, to teach you that man does not live on bread alone but on every word that comes from the mouth of the LORD." (Dt. 8:2)

Israel had just been shown God's care in the provision of manna for their hunger, yet they did not trust Him to give water for their thirst. They failed to see that they, not God, were on trial at Rephidim.

It was not the first or the last time that rebels against God reversed the situation to summon God to trial. Soon after World War II a play was produced in Germany, *The Sign of Jonah*, written by Guenter Rutenborn.[3] It appeared just as the German people were confronted by the horrors of the Holocaust. Belsen, Dakau, and Auschwitz had just been exposed—the concentration camps where the Nazis attempted the "final solution" of genocide.

The play posed the question, "Who is to blame?" Both the cast and the audience were drawn into the answer. But no one felt personally to blame. The housewife had struggled with rationing, the industrialist had kept up steel production, even the storm trooper had only been following his orders.

But in defending their innocence, the accused become accusers; they indict one another. They are all guilty—in differing degrees, some by words and some by silence, some in what they did, and some in what they failed to do. Under their guilt, they begin to use the same excuse: the blame is higher up—higher up in the army, higher up in the Party . . . higher up. "The real blame is much higher up. God is to blame. He is the One to be put on trial."

Who would not join in calling God to account for the misery of the world? Who indeed? The Bible answers: the one who lives by faith. The charges brought by Israel at Massah-Meribah show what the Bible calls "a sinful, unbelieving heart" (Heb. 3:12). Moses later warned Israel that they were not to put the Lord on trial as they did at Massah-Meribah (Dt. 6:16).

God is just, and is the Judge of all the earth. Israel had brought suit against Him; the case would be heard and judgment executed. God said to Moses, "Pass on before the people, taking with you some of the elders of Israel; and take in your hand the rod with which you struck the Nile, and go" (Ex. 17:5, RSV).

God's command brings drama to the scene. "Pass on before the people" may mean simply to go on ahead of them, but it also suggests that the people were aware of Moses' going.[4] Moses goes ahead to meet with God. He does not go as an accused criminal, but as the judge of Israel, bearing in his hand the rod of judgment. The stroke of that rod had turned the Nile River to blood, judging the gods of Egypt. With him Moses takes a number of the elders of Israel. They make up a court of judges and witnesses; their presence is necessary because of the legal formality of the situation.[5]

The rod of Moses was unique in power and authority, for it represented the judgment of God Himself. But a rod was the usual symbol of judicial authority. Our term "fascist" comes from the Roman *fasces*, the bundle of rods carried by the ancient Roman *lictors* to represent their office. A man found guilty of a crime in Israel could be sentenced to lie down before the judge and be beaten. The law limited the number of strokes he could receive to forty (Dt. 25:1-3).

The people well understood the symbol of the rod in the hand of Moses, their judge. They had seen the Nile run red when Moses brought down the rod on it. What judgment would come if Moses now lifted his rod against them? The prophet Isaiah saw the rod of God's judgment falling on the Gentiles:

> The LORD will cause men to hear his majestic voice
>   and will make them see his arm coming down
> with raging anger and consuming fire,
>   with cloudburst, thunderstorm and hail.
> The voice of the LORD will shatter Assyria;
>   with his scepter he will strike them down.
> Every stroke the LORD lays on them with his punishing
>   rod
>   will be to the music of tambourines and harps. . . .
>   (Is. 30:30-32)

At the command of God, Moses does raise the rod of judgment, but what follows is one of the most amazing incidents in Scripture. God said, "Behold, I will stand before thee there upon the rock in Horeb; and thou shalt smite the rock . . ." (Ex. 17:6, KJV).[6] In the Old Testament, God did not stand before men; men stood before God. In Deuteronomy the litigants in a law case were summoned to stand before the Lord and before the priests and judges (Dt. 19:17).

"Before the face" of Moses the judge, with his rod uplifted, stands the God of Israel. The Lord stands in the prisoner's dock. Moses cannot strike into the heart of God's *shekinah* glory. God commands that he strike the rock. But the rock is identified with God in the song of Moses: "Oh, praise the greatness of our God! He is the Rock, his works are perfect, and all his ways are just" (Dt. 32:3-4,31).

In the same Psalms that commemorate this Massah-Meribah trial, the name "Rock" is used for God: "the Rock of our salvation" (Ps. 78:15,20,35; 95:1). God, the Rock, identifies Himself with the rock by standing on it. Israel would put God on trial for breaking His covenant with their fathers. God stands in the place of the accused, and the penalty of the judgment is inflicted.

Is God, then, guilty? No, it is the people who are guilty. In rebellion they have refused to trust the faithfulness of God. Yet God, the Judge, bears the judgment; He receives the blow that their rebellion deserves. The law must be satisfied: if God's people are to be spared, He must bear their punishment.

In Rutenborn's play, God is tried, found guilty, and sentenced "to become a human being, a wanderer on earth, deprived of his rights, homeless, hungry, thirsty. He himself shall die! And lose a son, and suffer the agonies of fatherhood, and when at last he dies, he shall be disgraced and ridiculed."

So we rebels cry out in our rage. But God in His perfect righteousness has done more than the blasphemy of our cursing dares to demand. Isaiah declares, "In all their distress he too was distressed, and the angel of his presence saved them. In his love and mercy he redeemed them; he lifted them up and carried them all the days of old" (Is. 63:9).

Through the Old Testament there flows a stream of mercy that has its source at the throne of God. The Shepherd of Israel is the King of love, a God full of mercy and truth. The God who stands upon the rock is the God who spared Abraham's beloved son Isaac from the sacrificial knife with the promise, "The LORD will provide" (Gen. 22:14). God's redemption of His rebellious people must be more than an act of liberation; it must be an act of atoning love.

In His own Son, God came to bear our condemnation. What amazement, what awe Moses must have felt as he struck the rock of God! In God's due time that symbol was made reality. God "did not spare his own Son, but gave him up for us all" (Ro. 8:32). At the cross, the Son of God took the place of His condemned people and bore the stroke of judgment. Paul rightly says of Israel in the wilderness that they "drank from the spiritual rock that accompanied them, and that rock was Christ" (1 Cor. 10:4). John tells us that Jesus stood in the Temple on the last great day of the feast of tabernacles and called, "If anyone is thirsty, let him come to me. And let him drink, who believes in me. As the Scripture has said, streams of living water will flow from within him" (Jn. 7:38, NIV margin).

When Moses struck the rock, a stream of life-giving water poured out into the desert. When Jesus was crucified, John tells us that blood and water poured from His side (Jn. 19:34). In reminding us of the water as well as the blood, John recalls for us the cry of Jesus at the feast. At Calvary there flowed from His heart the streams of living water. The water that Christ gives is the water of the Holy Spirit (Jn. 7:38-39). The breath of the risen Christ symbolized the gift of the Spirit (Jn. 20:22-23); so does the water that flowed with the blood of the Crucified. The Spirit of life is given through Christ's death.

We do not wonder that Moses was judged severely for striking the rock a second time, when he had been told to speak to it (Num. 20:7-13). Only once, at His appointed time, does God bear the stroke of our doom.

The God who is the Rock of Israel is the Savior, the God of mercy who bears His own judgment for the sin of His people. The people had cried in the accusation of unbelief, "Is the LORD among us or not?" Yes, the Lord was among them, among them in a way they could not have imagined. There He stood upon the rock; not only among them, but in their place, bearing their condemnation. Before God gave His covenant at Sinai, He pledged His presence at Calvary.

The history of God's redemption moves from grace to grace. The grace of God's promise to the patriarchs and the grace of His exodus deliverance point toward the ultimate grace to come in Jesus Christ. This is apparent in the prophetic overview of the history of redemption found in Deuteronomy (30:1-10). Moses commanded the tribes of Israel to divide into two vast assemblies after they entered the land. Half the tribes were to assemble on Mount Gerizim and recite all the blessings God would bring upon them as they kept His covenant (Dt. 27:12; 28:1-14). The other half were to stand on Mount Ebal and recite the curses that would rest on them if they were disobedient (Dt. 27:13; 28:15-68). We then learn that these were not simply two possibilities, but that both would be realized. At the beginning of chapter 30, we see that Moses declared what would come to pass after both the blessings and the curses were poured out. The people would then be scattered in captivity among the nations, but as they turned again to the Lord, he would not only restore them to their land, but "The LORD your God will circumcise your hearts and the hearts of your descendants, so that you may love him with all your heart and with all your soul, and live" (Dt. 30:6).

This structure spans the whole of biblical history. Israel did, indeed, receive the blessings God had promised. When King Solomon blessed the people at the dedication of the Temple, he declared, "Praise be to the LORD, who has given rest to his people Israel just as he promised. Not one word has failed of all the good promises he gave through his servant Moses" (1 Ki. 8:56).

This same King Solomon, however, built shrines to other gods in Jerusalem to accommodate the idolatry of his heathen wives. After his death, his kingdom was divided. Israel in the north and then Judah in the south sank into idolatry and apostasy. The prophets warned of the rising storm of the judgments to come, but the people mocked their doomsaying. The Assyrians destroyed Samaria and carried Israel into captivity. The Babylonian empire brought the same fate on Judah. Jerusalem was put to the torch, its walls broken down, the Temple destroyed. Judgment, total and devastating, had followed blessing.

Yet God's promises were not forgotten. The prophets who warned of disaster looked forward to a time to come: the "latter days" after the blessing and the curse. God would spare a remnant, restore them to the land from their captivity, and renew His covenant with them in a glory that could not be imagined.

The outline of the history of Israel in Deuteronomy 30 became the burden of the prophets. They proclaimed God's judgment, but after judgment, the glory of God's work of redemption, climaxed in the last days. The royal grace of God, the Rock, would triumph in the salvation of His people. God's triumph would be the work of a greater Prophet than Moses; it would be the work of the Lord's Anointed.

NOTES:
1. The verb for God's *showing* the tree to Moses is the root of the term *torah*, God's law as a pointer, showing the way. The sign no less than the command is appointed by God.
2. For a scholarly description of the use of this term, see H.B. Huffmon, "The Covenant Lawsuit in the Prophets," *Journal of Biblical Literature*, LXXVII, pages 285ff; B. Gemser, "The RIB or Controversy Pattern" in *Wisdom in Israel and the Ancient Near East* (*Vetus Testamentum*, Supplement III, Leiden: 1955).
3. Guenter Rutenborn, *The Sign of Jonah* (New York: Thomas Nelson and Sons, 1960).
4. The same phrase is used to describe the priests who carried the ark of the covenant through the Jordan before the people of Israel (Josh. 3:6). It is used of the Lord's passing by Moses in the cleft of the rock (Ex. 34:6). God did not simply go on ahead of Moses, but passed by to go ahead, covering Moses with His hand as He did so.
5. The situation is different when Moses is commanded to speak to the rock at a later time. Then Israel was to be assembled, and the miracle was to occur before their eyes (Num. 20:8). But the elders were not required as witnesses; Moses is to bear, but not to use, the rod, and the setting is no longer that of a trial.
6. The NIV translation weakens the force of the Hebrew by omitting, for stylistic reasons, the emphatic "Behold." The most natural translation is that God stood *upon* the rock, not *beside* it. The preposition may mean *beside* when describing the position of a person standing in relation to one seated or lying face down; the sense of "over" is still present.

7
THE LORD'S ANOINTED

Warriors of the Covenant

Joshua, the commander of the armies of Israel, stood alone, looking at the walls of Jericho. He knew well the fortified cities of Canaan; years before he had scouted the land. Those long years ago Israel had refused to follow his courageous counsel; they had turned back to wander for forty years in the desert. Now the years of wandering were over. Moses was dead, but the Lord who had parted the Red Sea to lead Israel out of Egypt had parted the Jordan River to lead them into the Promised Land. The manna had ceased; they were now to live on the land the Lord had given them.

As Joshua looked up at the walls and towers of Jericho, the charge that God had given him rang in his heart: "No one will be able to stand up against you all the days of your life. As I was with Moses, so I will be with you; I will never leave you nor forsake you. . . . Be strong and courageous. Do not be terrified; do not be discouraged, for the LORD your God will be with you wherever you go" (Josh. 1:5,9).

Joshua had the pledge of God's presence, and the charge to keep God's commandments. What strategy should he now follow? How was Jericho to be assaulted? As Joshua pondered, he was startled to see a warrior confronting him with a drawn sword. Joshua's hand went to his own sword as he advanced to challenge the stranger: "Are you for us or for our enemies?"

"No, but as Commander of the army of the LORD I have now come" (Josh. 5:14, NKJV).

Joshua fell on his face before the Lord: "What message does my Lord have for his servant?" At the burning bush in Sinai, the Lord had told Moses to take off his sandals. Now He told Joshua to do the same thing: "The place where you are standing is holy."

The Lord had promised to be with Joshua. He now revealed His presence. The Lord came bearing the sword as the Commander, not simply of the armies of Israel but of the hosts of heaven. The commander Joshua met his supreme Commander. It was well that Joshua fell down before Him. No man is prepared to confront the drawn sword of the Lord. God once met Moses on his way back to Egypt and threatened his life until his sons were circumcised (Ex. 4:24).

Under the leadership of Joshua, Israel had just been circumcised at Gilgal (Josh. 5:2-9). There they had celebrated the Passover, reminding them of the threat of death against the firstborn of Israel, as well as of the Egyptians. Joshua might well have feared that the Lord would come against him as an Adversary to engage him in combat, as He had engaged Jacob at the Jabbok. Joshua did not need a burning bush to remind him that the Holy One of Israel is a consuming fire (Mal. 3:2).

The Lord was the Commander, not Joshua. God did not come down to do Joshua's bidding; He could not be summoned to provide military support as the Commander of an auxiliary battalion of angels. Rather, if it were not for His own free mercy and the grace of His covenant, the Lord would indeed stand as the Adversary of Joshua and Israel.

Yet the Lord had not come with His sword drawn against Israel but against the wickedness of the Canaanites. The cup of their iniquity was full; the day of their judgment had arrived (Gen. 15:16; Lev. 18:24-25). The Lord did not bring Israel into the land as invading conquerors, but as avenging angels, the executors of His judgment. The doom of Canaan must be compared to the doom of Sodom and Gomorrah: an anticipation in history of God's final judgment.

The Lord is the Commander; He came to carry out His own will, His own plan. He came as a Warrior because His mission was to be the Captain of Israel's salvation. He spoke to Joshua to instruct him in the divine strategy by which Jericho would be taken. His sword of judgment was drawn on behalf of His people. Joshua could be assured that the Lord was on his side because he was on the Lord's side. "If God is for us, who can be against us?" (Ro. 8:31).

Before the first campaign of Israel under Joshua, before the years of struggle that gave Israel secure possession of the land, God appeared as the Divine Warrior. If the people feared Him, they needed to fear none other. Jesus before His crucifixion said, "Now is the time for judgment on this world; now the prince of this world will be driven out" (Jn. 12:31).

The language of battle and victory fills the Scripture, but not because bloodshed is taken lightly or the weapons of war prized. Rather, the terminology of war is applied to the ultimate struggle between the Lord of Hosts and the "prince of this world." In the holy war to which Israel is summoned, this struggle is foreshadowed with chilling clarity. Israel fights not whom they will but only those whom God's judgment has marked for destruction.

This explains why Israel was not free to spare those whom God had doomed. When King Saul spared Agag, the king of Amalek, Samuel the prophet pronounced God's verdict against Agag and executed God's vengeance with his own hand (1 Sam. 15:33). Because Saul had rejected God's explicit commandment, he was rejected as a theocratic king. For the same reason, it was a crime of blasphemous proportions for Israel to take for themselves the spoil of the city or people that God had devoted to destruction. Such disobedience perverted the judicial role of Israel, and made them to be murderers for their own profit like the aggressor empires of their day.

Likewise, when Jericho was to fall to the armies of Israel, it was to be totally destroyed, with the exception of the household of Rahab, who had shown her faith in the God of Israel by protecting the spies Joshua had sent to gather information. Achan, a warrior of Israel, was a victim of his own covetousness; he supposed that he could hide a small treasure taken from the city: a beautiful robe from Babylonia, two hundred shekels of silver, and a wedge of gold. God's judgment was swift. Israel suffered disastrous defeat at the small city of Ai; not until Achan's theft had been exposed and his sin judged did victory return to the armies of Israel.

We may find the concept of a holy war difficult to accept, in part because of the way in which Islam has taken over the concept from the Old Testament. We react against the proclamation of *jihad* by the mullahs of Islamic fundamentalism in Iran. Yet God's commission to Israel was grounded in His righteous judgment against sin.

God's judgments are still visited on human wickedness: Hitler's Reich went down in flames. We live, however, in the time when God's ultimate judgment is postponed—postponed so that men might repent and receive the mercy of

God revealed at Calvary (Ro. 2:3-6). God gave the sword to Israel to use in His name. Jesus withheld the sword from the church (Mt. 26:52; Jn. 18:11,36). The New Testament recognizes the God-given right of the state to use the sword (Ro. 13:4), but God has not appointed the state to be the executor of His total justice. That final judgment is given to Jesus Christ, and awaits His return (2 Thess. 1:7-10). The theocratic law of Israel as the people of God is continued in the church, but transformed through Christ's fulfillment. Its sanctions are spiritual, not physical.

The spiritual nature of Christ's battle and victory was foreshadowed in the conquest of Jericho. The Lord, appearing as Commander, instructed Joshua in the remarkable assault on the city. The soldiers were not to lay siege to the city or build mounds against its walls. No battering rams were to be constructed. Instead, a religious procession was to be ordered. The army was to march in silence around the walls of the city. Following them came the priests with the ark of the covenant, blowing on seven trumpets. At Sinai, the sound of trumpets had announced the presence of God (Ex. 19:13). At the climax of Israel's sacred calendar, the Year of Jubilee was to be heralded with the blast of the silver trumpet. The ark represented the presence of the Lord with Israel, and the sound of the trumpet announced His presence in judgment.

Each day the solemn procession stirred the dust around the walls of Jericho. By the sixth day, no doubt, the inhabitants were mocking the apparently futile demonstration. On the seventh day the long march began early in the morning. Seven times Israel marched around Jericho. When the trumpets blew at the end of the seventh lap, the army shouted, and the walls of Jericho crumbled in their place. Then the soldiers of Israel swept into the demoralized city and destroyed it.

Israel used the sword at God's command, but it was not their prowess in battle that gave them the victory. The battle was the Lord's, and the victory His. This remains the theme of the history of Israel's warfare. The theme is replayed with countless variations, but the message is the same. Salvation is of the Lord. He is in charge, the Commander who stood before Joshua.

At the sound of the trumpet of God, every wall shall fall. The apostle Paul once wore the sword to persecute the church of Christ. The Lord, however, brought Paul to his face on the road to Damascus; his sword was abandoned. But he was not without weapons. Rather, he rejoiced in the weapons of the Spirit for the spiritual struggle in which he was engaged.

> For though we live in the world, we do not wage war as the world does. The weapons we fight with are not the weapons of the world. On the contrary, they have divine power to demolish strongholds. We demolish arguments and every pretension that sets itself up against the knowledge of God, and we take captive every thought to make it obedient to Christ. (2 Cor. 10:3-5)

Paul was a herald of the gospel. He blew on the gospel trumpet and saw the citadels of evil fall. Vividly he described the power of his ministry among the Gentiles. He was like a priest presiding over the offering up of the Gentiles to God (Ro. 15:16). Paul's missionary journeys were indeed a triumphal procession, but the triumph was not his, but Christ's (2 Cor. 2:14). He was Christ's captive, chained to His chariot as Christ rode in triumph.

The promise given to Joshua as the Lord stood before him was a promise that is now fulfilled through Christ's victory over the principalities and the powers. The Lord who promised Joshua that He would never leave or forsake him (Josh. 1:5) is the same Lord who said to His disciples, "Lo, I am with you always, even to the end of the age" (Mt. 28:20, NKJV).

In the rich symbolism of Joshua's meeting with the Commander, we have an anticipation of the whole history of redemption seen in the format of holy war. Jesus comes as the Prince and Commander, the Lord of Hosts who will conquer and reign. Yet the figure of Joshua is also significant. His name bears witness to the fact that the Lord saves. He is the chosen commander of the people of God; he stands in the place of Moses as the servant of the Lord. As such, he prepares us for Jesus, his greater namesake.

The role of Joshua as the military leader of the people of God prepares the way for the later judges and kings of Israel. He anticipates, therefore, the role of Christ as the Lord's Anointed, the Son of David, who is the Savior and Deliverer of the people of God. Jesus fulfills both sides of God's covenant. He is the Lord, the Divine Warrior, who comes for the salvation of His own. He is also the Servant, the Lord's Anointed, through whom the victory is won. Joshua and his successors, the judges and kings of Israel, fight the battles of the Lord through the long centuries of Israel's warfare in the land. Their struggles are recorded, not to describe their military genius, but to show how God used them to deliver Israel. They all foreshadow a greater Deliverer and Savior to come.

The record of the book of Judges clearly describes the history of God's rule over His wayward people. Initially they fail to destroy or drive out all the inhabitants of the land. Those who remain become a source of corruption for Israel. Again and again they forget the Lord and lapse into idolatry and immorality, imitating the very sins for which God judged the Canaanites. In judgment, God then delivers them up to their enemies. The tribes are divided, the people are enslaved. Stripped of the weapons they might use for their defense, they are forced to yield the fruit of the land to their oppressors. Driven by desperation, they cry to the Lord, and He raises up judges to deliver them and to provide periods of order and areas of peace (Jdg. 3:9,15; 6:7-8,11).

God's mercy appears in His continual sending of saviors and judges. When His people again cry to Him after repeatedly returning to their apostasy, we are told that "his soul could no longer endure the misery of Israel" (Jdg. 10:16, NKJV). Even before they repent under the exploitation of the Philistines, the Lord begins His work of deliverance by sending His Angel to announce the birth of Samson.

It may seem strange that the birth of such an ineffectual judge as Samson should be introduced by a full chapter describing two appearances of the Angel of the Lord, first to the wife of Manoah and then to the couple together (Jdg. 13). Indeed, the literary artistry of the Samson stories and their dramatic power may also puzzle us. Why should so much attention be given to a judge who squandered his enduement and ignored his calling? Is the history of Samson given for its entertainment value? Is Samson an Israeli Rambo, a Superman for a biblical comic strip?

The answer appears in the witness that Samson provided, almost in spite of himself, to his role as a savior of the people of God. Samson was called to be a Nazirite, one consecrated to God in a special sense, set apart by his vow to abstain from strong drink. His untrimmed hair marked his vow in the eyes of his tribe and of the Philistine overlords. In the days of Samson, the nation of Israel was not only oppressed but demoralized. When Samson avenged a Philistine atrocity, his own tribe rebuked him. "Don't you realize that the Philistines are rulers over us? What have you done to us?" (Jdg. 15:11). Threatened by a Philistine army, his own people gladly tied him up and handed him over to the enemy.

Under Deborah, the woman judge of Israel, the people had offered themselves willingly in the day of battle (Jdg. 5:2,9). In the time of Samson, however, that willingness to trust in the Lord for victory was gone. God had shown that He could deliver Israel with an army of willing volunteers; He had also shown that He could save with as few as three hundred dedicated warriors. Gideon's tiny force had startled and routed a great invading army of Midianites.

But when the Spirit of God came upon Samson, the Lord showed that He had no need for even three hundred. He could deliver by one. Bound by his own nation, delivered over to the Gentiles, without followers or weapons, Samson overwhelmed a thousand Philistines. His weapon lay within his reach when he burst his bonds: the jawbone of an ass (not quite as bizarre as it might seem; jawbones fitted with flint knives were used as primitive weapons).

Samson's cry of victory was an outrageous pun. The Hebrew term for "ass" was the same as the word for "heap." Samson's cry uses the same term three times in a row: "With the jawbone of a 'heap' [ass], heap heaps." ("With the jawbone of an ass, I have slain a thousand men.") The pun can't be translated, of course. "With the jawbone of an ass I assailed my assailants"—that doesn't quite bring it off.

In the next instant, Samson's bitter humor turned to desperate prayer. Collapsing with exhaustion and dehydration, he flung away the jawbone[1] and cried to God for water. God provided a spring in the hollow place of Lehi ("Jawbone"). From the place of death and judgment, God opened a spring of life.

In Psalm 110 David described the triumph of the Messiah, who would thirst after the carnage of battle:

He shall judge among the nations,
He shall fill with . . . bodies,
He shall execute the heads of many countries.
He shall drink of the brook by the wayside;
Therefore He shall lift up the head.[2]

The apostle Paul reflects on the exaltation of Christ to God's right hand predicted in this Psalm (Eph. 1:20-22). He meditates on the spiritual triumph of Christ as the gospel reaches the nations. Using the vocabulary of this Psalm, Paul affirms, not that Christ fills with bodies but that He fills the body, the church. His head is lifted up, for He is head over all things for the church (Eph. 1:22).

Perhaps the weakness of Samson the strongman helps us to distinguish between the man himself and his calling: the role that the Lord appointed for him to fulfill. Samson held an office in Israel: he held God's appointment to a function that was defined by God's call and recognized, at least in retrospect, by the people he served. This is how his career is summarized: "And he judged Israel twenty years in the days of the Philistines" (Jdg. 15:20, NKJV).

As we have seen, the appointed roles of God's servants point forward to their fulfillment in God's final Servant, Jesus Christ. They have a symbolic function, providing a key to the way in which the historical narratives of the Old Testament demonstrate types of the work of Christ. In spite of Samson's abuse of the endowment of power that was his, God used him to show His power to save.

Samson's physical power was the gift of the Spirit, equipping him for combat as a champion of the Lord. In battle he was invincible. Yet he never led Israel against the enemy, nor did he seek to establish God's Kingdom according to His promise. The strongman killed a lion barehanded, but he did it on the way to take a Philistine wife in disobedience to God's law. He killed thirty men of Ashkalon, but he did so to collect their garments to pay off a wager. He wrenched the gates of Gaza from their sockets and carried them to a mountain top, but he performed that exploit to escape from a trap that had been set for him while he spent the night with a harlot in the Philistine city.

Samson maintained the external separation of his vow as a Nazirite, but as John Milton observed in *Samson Agonistes*:

> But what availed this temperance, not complete
> Against another object more enticing?
> What boots it at one gate to make defense
> And at another to let in the foe
> Effeminately vanquished!

At the last the shell of his outward dedication to the Lord fell away. His progressive compromise led him to confide his secret to Delilah. His hair was cut away, and his supernatural strength was gone. Betrayed into the hands of his Philistine enemies, he was helpless. He had lived for the lust of the eye; now he was blinded by the Philistines. His appetites had made him captive to the women he sought. Now he was put to grinding grain, made to serve in the role of a woman slave. Sport was his delight; now the Philistines made sport at his expense. They celebrated their triumph in the temple of their god Dagon, and had Samson brought before them that they might mock his blind helplessness.

But God had not deserted Samson. In prison his hair had grown—the mark of his Nazirite separation to the God of the covenant. Samson was led into the temple through jeering thousands. They began a victory chant that was echoed by a vast crowd on the roof above, looking down into the courtyard. They demanded tricks, offered tests of strength to show his weakness. Samson endured the mockery. Then he realized that he stood in the center of the temple, near the great wooden columns set on stone bases, columns that supported the roof. Samson said to the lad who led him, "Put me where I can feel the pillars that support the temple, so that I may lean against them."

Then Samson prayed, "O Lord Jehovah, remember me, I pray thee, and strengthen me, I pray thee, only this once, O God, that I may be avenged for one of my two eyes" (Jdg. 16:28, ASV margin). With one hand against each of the pillars, Samson bowed himself and thrust them apart, forcing them off their bases. One last prayer was on his lips: "Let me die with the Philistines!" The roof with its vast crowd collapsed on Samson and the mass of people below. The account concludes: "Thus he killed many more when he died than while he lived" (Jdg. 16:30).

The narrative does nothing to make a saint of Samson. He died seeking vengeance, and the bitterness of his final words seems a bit much even for the translators, who feel that the most literal translation cannot be right. How could Samson bring down this destruction on himself and the Philistines to avenge just *one* of his two eyes! Yet the words fit both the anger of Samson and his love of deadly riddles; he would return the mockery of his enemies on their heads.

Can the tragic life of Samson point us forward to Jesus Christ? If we catch the force of the narrative, we will see that it must. Clearly the story of Samson is not told in order that young men might emulate him. The account is often heavily censored for Sunday school use! But neither is Samson presented as a counter-example, one who shows the folly of sin and the need for repentance. His death is not presented as a divine judgment, nor do his last words confess sin and seek forgiveness.

To be sure, we may well contrast the story of Samson

with that of Samuel, whose birth was also prophesied. But the thrust of the Samson narrative is not to prepare for such a contrast. Rather, it is to show how God can bring judgment on the foes of His people through one man, equipped by the Holy Spirit. Samson's weakness and sins only serve to heighten the gap between his own life and his calling as a judge of Israel. We are not called to admire Samson's virtues, but to recognize his faith. He knew that his strength was God's gift, and he died in faith, calling on God to judge His enemies (Heb. 11:13,32-34).

Jesus Christ is the mighty Savior foreshadowed by the symbolism of Samson's calling. In contrast to Samson (and to John the Baptist), Jesus is separated to God not by an outward nonconformity, but by an inward holiness. He is a spiritual Nazirite, called by the Father from His mother's womb. His distinctiveness is shown by His perfect obedience, obedience acknowledged by His Father's voice from heaven (Mt. 3:17; 17:5).

Samson was endued with the Holy Spirit, marking the pattern that would be realized in Christ as the Bearer of the Spirit. Like Samson, Jesus was bound by the leaders of His own people and handed over to the Gentile oppressors. Like Samson, too, Jesus was mocked as helpless; not blinded, to be sure, but blindfolded, he was made the sport of His captors. Jesus willingly gave up His life. In His death He wrought a deliverance that exceeded the deliverances of His life.

The typical aspects of Samson's life are not to be sought in the similarity of details. The gates of Gaza, removed by Samson to the heights of Hebron, cannot be identified directly with the gates of death. They are not in themselves symbolic. The structure that grounds the typology of the Old Testament narratives is the continuity of God's work of redemption as it unfolds through history. The role of the

judge as a divinely endued and appointed deliverer anticipates the Judge who is yet to come.

The invincible might of Samson in the power of the
Spirit does point us toward the final revelation of that principle in the victory of Jesus Christ. We are told of Samson's
removal of the gates of Gaza so we may understand that no
power can contain the Spirit-endued champion of the people
of God. His exploit, therefore, does foreshadow, dimly but
truly, Christ's victory when death cannot hold Him.

The rejection of Samson by his tribe fits the pattern of
the rejected servant of the Lord, a pattern that extends
through the history of redemption. From the blood of Abel
to that of the last prophet who suffered for his calling, the
story of God's servants is one of rejection.

On the other hand, the pattern again and again continues with a reverse twist. God not only uses and blesses His
rejected servants; He even makes use of their rejection to
further His purposes. The Danites handed Samson over to
the Philistines, but in so doing they unleashed the judgment
of God upon their enemies. The theme of victory through
apparent defeat is not accidental in the story of Samson. It is
another instance of the overruling power of God's deliverance. His strength is made perfect in weakness.

In the period of the judges, God raised up warriors of
the covenant to deliver His people from their oppressors.
Samson showed that the Lord could deliver through a solitary champion. Samson, however, was no real leader of
Israel. After the stormy period of the judges, it was through
the king, and especially King David, that a deliverer was
raised up who was both a champion and a leader.

The Warrior King
The kingship was inaugurated, at the demand of the people,
by Samuel, the greatest of the judges of Israel. Samuel lived

as a boy with Eli, the priest of the Lord, in the sanctuary. In the dark ages of Israel's disunity there was little revelation from the Lord. The Lord spoke to Samuel, making him His prophet. Samuel led and judged Israel as a minister of God's word and a man of prayer.

Samuel's leadership stood in stark contrast with the fashion in which Samson fought the Philistines. Samuel did not fight with the jawbone of an ass, but with the sacrifice of a lamb. He called on the people to repent of their sin, to put away their idols, and to pray to the Lord for victory over the Philistine oppressors. They asked him to pray as they went to battle against the invaders. Samuel did so; as the Philistines made their charge, Samuel was offering sacrifice to the Lord (1 Sam. 7:10). God disrupted the Philistine advance with the thunder of His judgment; the Israelites were given the victory. Samuel praised God and set up the memorial of Ebenezer ("the stone of help").

The people, however, were not content that prayer should be their defense. They recognized that Samuel's own sons were not heirs to his prophetic gifts, and they did not look to the Lord to raise up another Samuel to lead them. No, they wanted to have a king like the other nations. They preferred to have their defense institutionalized. Samuel was distressed at the people's rebelliousness, but God instructed him to grant their request, warning them of the price they would pay for an earthly kingship.

Saul, the first king of Israel, brought initial victories, but failed miserably in his calling to be God's anointed. He just couldn't believe that God was able to deliver by few; when he saw his voluntary army dwindling, he offered sacrifice himself rather than waiting for the delayed coming of Samuel (1 Sam. 13:9). Then, when the Lord charged him to obliterate the Amalekites as an action of divine judgment, he spared the best of the sheep and oxen as well as Agag, the king.

Samuel withdrew from Saul to indicate that the Lord had rejected him (1 Sam. 15). At God's command, Samuel anointed David, chosen of God to succeed Saul as king of Israel (1 Sam. 16).

In the accounts of David, the warrior king of Israel, we are given the fullest anticipation of the victory of the coming Savior. Like Samson and other judges, David was a fighter, courageous and skillful in battle. Unlike Samson, he was also a leader, considerate of his troops, grateful for their service. Like Samuel, he was a man of prayer, who heeded the word of the Lord. While David was not a prophet in the sense that Samuel was, he did receive revelation from God (Acts 2:30-31), and was the inspired author of many of the Psalms.

In the Old Testament record of the service of King David to the Lord, we read the story of Jesus. The ministry of David's greater Son is foreshadowed in the life of David. This is apparent in the trials and suffering that David endured precisely because he was the Lord's anointed. The theme of the righteous servant of the Lord enduring scorn and affliction for the Lord's sake is eloquently described in the Psalms of David:

> For I endure scorn for your sake,
>> and shame covers my face.
> I am a stranger to my brothers,
>> an alien to my own mother's sons;
> for zeal for your house consumes me,
>> and the insults of those who insult you fall on me.
> When I weep and fast,
>> I must endure scorn;
> when I put on sackcloth,
>> people make sport of me.
> Those who sit at the gate mock me,
>> and I am the song of the drunkards. (Ps. 69:7-12)

David's experience of suffering for the Lord's sake arose in part from the enmity of the Philistines and the surrounding nations. David recalled in Psalm 56 the experience he had in Gath when he sought refuge from Saul's jealous pursuit in the Philistine city:

> Be merciful to me, O God, for men hotly pursue me;
> > all day long they press their attack.
> My slanderers pursue me all day long;
> > many are attacking me in their pride.
> When I am afraid,
> > I will trust in you.   (Ps. 56:1-3)

Only by the most humiliating performance did David make good his escape on that occasion. He played the madman, drooling in his beard, clawing like an animal on the gates of the city. Achish, the king of Gath, on the reasonable assumption that his court was adequately supplied with fools, ordered David's release (1 Sam. 21:14-15).

David's greatest afflictions, however, did not come from the Gentile enemies but from his own people. King Saul became insanely jealous of David's exploits and his popularity with the people. While David was playing on the harp to calm the tormented king, he narrowly missed being pinned to the wall by the spear Saul suddenly threw at him. One narrow escape followed another. On one occasion, Michal, Saul's daughter and David's wife, warned her husband to flee, and prepared a dummy figure in bed to throw off pursuit. David became an outlaw in the wilderness of Judah; a band of wronged and desperate men gathered around him. Saul's pursuit of David on that occasion came within yards of success. As the troops of the king closed in one day, the sudden news of a Philistine invasion drew off Saul to the discharge of his proper royal duty.

The stories are vividly told. We see Saul turning aside to relieve himself in a cave, the very cave in which David and a band of his men were hiding. David's lieutenants saw this as a God-given opportunity to dispatch the murderous king and bring an end to all their problems. But David would not hear a word of it. He stealthily cut off the corner of the robe that Saul had tossed aside, but he would not touch the king. Even that minor alteration to Saul's wardrobe concerned David: "The LORD forbid that I should do such a thing to my master, the LORD's anointed, or lift my hand against him" (1 Sam. 24:6).

When Saul was at a safe distance a little later, David displayed the swatch of Saul's robe and gained a respite by shaming Saul into recognizing David's goodwill.

From the crucible of his persecution by Saul and later from his own rebellious son Absalom, David poured out his heart to the Lord in Psalms of lament. He refused to take vengeance against Saul into his own hands. His respect for Saul's anointing as the king of Israel was, of course, also a recognition of his own anointing by the Lord to succeed Saul. But David did not take his own anointing as a license to seize the throne by destroying Saul. Rather, he committed his cause to God, and trusted God to judge His enemies and to keep His promise.

The afflictions and trials of David cast the shadow of death over the valley where David confessed that the Lord was his Shepherd. David's victories were victories of faith. We see this dedication of David's faith at the very beginning of his battles, his encounter with the Philistine champion Goliath. It was his faith, his zeal for the honor of the Lord of Hosts, that moved him to volunteer to fight the giant.

We read in the story how his father sent him to the battle front with food for his three brothers and their comrades. There he heard the boasting challenge of Goliath, and seemed amazed that no one was ready to accept it and put an end to the blasphemy. Eliab, his older brother, showed more than the usual scorn for a young sibling: "Why have you come down here? And with whom did you leave those few sheep in the desert? I know how conceited you are and how wicked your heart is; you came down only to watch the battle" (1 Sam. 17:28).

Plainly, Eliab was stung by David's zeal. In the setting of the narrative, however, we see that David was acting as the Lord's anointed (1 Sam. 16:12-13). The Spirit of the Lord rested on him in virtue of his calling. The narrative reminds us of David's anointing by repeating the description of David as a youth "ruddy and handsome." That phrase is used of David as Goliath saw him; it was also used of David's appearance when Samuel anointed him to be king (1 Sam. 16:12; cf. 17:42). Although he was indeed young, he was anointed with the Spirit. Goliath saw him advancing without armor, with just a staff in his hand. The champion from Gath was insulted: "Am I a dog, that you come at me with sticks?"

He cursed David by his gods. "Come here," he said, "and I'll give your flesh to the birds of the air and the beasts of the field" (1 Sam. 17:44). David was no more intimidated by Goliath's bluster than by his size or his weapons. "You come to me with a sword, with a spear, and with a javelin. But I come to you in the name of the LORD of Hosts, the God of the armies of Israel, whom you have defied" (1 Sam. 17:45, NKJV).

The God of the armies of Israel is the God of the hosts of heaven. He has all power in heaven and on earth. David's courage is the courage of faith. No matter that Goliath is nine feet tall and advances with weaponry like a battle tank. His opponent is not a stripling with a staff but the Lord's anointed, endued with the Spirit of God. To be sure, David's ballistic missile proves technologically superior to Goliath's fifteen-pound spearhead, but it is God's blessing that gives David the victory.

The episodes of David's wilderness years show the testings and triumphs of David's faith. There are days of depression when David despairs of relief from Saul's pursuit. Yet again and again the Lord renews David's hope. At the end of the account of David's life, a summary is given of some of the exploits of David's warriors. They are memorialized in their rank as heroes, the knights of David's round table.

One of the records in this hall of fame shows clearly the meaning of devotion in the battles of the king (2 Sam. 23:13-17). David's men were fiercely loyal to their chief. That loyalty was carried to the pitch of devotion. Strong loyalty is not uncommon today among guerilla bands hunted by oppressive regimes. We often encounter it in ersatz form in the world of sports. It is not enough to be mildly favorable to a local sports team. One must be obsessed such as a "Phillies Phanatic."

The story of devotion in the annals of the king has its setting in the earliest days of David's reign as king of Israel. After Saul's death, David had been recognized as king by his own tribe of Judah. Seven years later he was inaugurated as king over all Israel. The Philistines, hearing of his enthronement, moved against him. They had defeated Saul, and they meant to capture David and nip his kingdom in the bud.

The Philistine army moved far into the territory of Judah and occupied Bethlehem with a strong garrison (2 Sam. 5:17-18). David, who did not yet have a full army to defend his kingdom, took refuge at a familiar strong point in the wilderness of Judah, a bastion that he knew well from his days as an outlaw pursued by Saul. He was joined there by loyal volunteers, including, no doubt, many veterans of his outlaw past. It was the harvest season, a poor time for recruiting, but among the day's volunteers there appeared three men especially devoted to the king's cause.

It was hot under the wilderness sun, and in the hearing of the three, David murmured a deep desire, "Oh, that someone would get me a drink of water from the well near the gate of Bethlehem!" (2 Sam. 23:15). There was, of course, a spring at David's stronghold. No camp would be possible without it. But David longed for water from Bethlehem, the Philistine garrison. Bethlehem was David's hometown, as the Philistines were well aware. Perhaps David had nostalgic memories of hot afternoons like this in his boyhood when he had come in from the fields to ask a drink from a friend drawing water at the well.

But surely there was more than nostalgia in David's desire. He was God's anointed king, enthroned over all of Israel, yet the Philistine army occupied the very town of his birth. Would the Lord deliver Bethlehem again into his hands? Could the Philistines be defeated? David was soon to put that question to the Lord (2 Sam. 5:19).

The three warriors heard their king's wish. They exchanged looks, belted on their swords, picked up a pitcher, and set off across the wilderness for Bethlehem.

Old Testament narratives are spare indeed in providing descriptions of the settings of action. Even the deeds of heroes are not romantically embroidered. We are not told when or where the three swordsmen first met opposition, or what outpost of the Philistine garrison first challenged them. But we are told that they broke through the Philistine lines and entered Bethlehem. Did they fight their way up the hill to the gate of the city? If not, they surely had to fight when they entered.

The city gate would have been the command post of the Philistine garrison. The open area there was the place where the troops would be mustered. Did a woman of the town draw the water for them? Did one soldier draw it while the others defended him? We are not told. Clearly, escaping from the town with the water would be the harder fight. Perhaps hardest of all was their return across the wilderness after their combat, *carrying* the water instead of drinking it!

David had not commanded this raid. He had not even asked for volunteers for it. These men would surely have obeyed the king's command. They would just as surely have volunteered if David had asked for men to step forward for a dangerous mission. But David had only expressed a wish, as the language makes clear. The king's wish was their command.

The community of God's covenant is bound by cords deeper than loyalty. The ties that bind God's people together are the ties of mutual devotion. Charles Colson has described the brotherhood of the Washington Fellowship that pointed him to the love of Christ. That movement takes to heart the charge of the apostle Peter, "Love the brotherhood" (1 Pet. 2:17). In the church of Jesus Christ leaders are not arm twisters. They are encouraged and supported by the cheerful service of men and women who do not have to be asked.

The warriors may have been near exhaustion as they returned to the camp and sought out David, their king. He had wished for water from the well of Bethlehem. They gave him the pitcher. David's reaction has puzzled some readers of the story. He took the pitcher and slowly poured the water out on the ground. The men saw a little puddle as the water sank into the parched earth. The slanting rays of the sun quickly dried the spot.

Was David thoughtless, spurning the sacrifice of his soldiers? Quite to the contrary. David cherished their devotion. He would not drink the water because it was too precious to drink. "Far be it from me, O LORD, to do this!" he said. "Is it not the blood of men who went at the risk of their lives?" (2 Sam. 23:17). David poured the water out as an offering to the Lord. David's humility points to his devotion to the Lord.

There have always been self-styled shepherds of God's flock who have exploited God's people for their own profit: eating the meat, dressing in the wool, but not caring for the flock (Ezk. 34:1-10). Few can forget the video image of Jim Jones in Guyana, sitting in a chair on a wooden platform while his followers drank poison at his word. A pastor need not build a People's Temple with the insane egotism of Jim Jones in order to lord it over those entrusted to him rather than serving them.

David did not accept the sacrificial gift of the water as his due. Rather, he received it as that which was given to God. The apostle Paul in the same way speaks of a gift sent to him by the Philippians as "a fragrant offering, an acceptable sacrifice, pleasing to God" (Phil. 4:18). No doubt by the very act of consecrating the water to the Lord, David encouraged his men to understand their own calling. They served the Lord God of Israel. The water was not the trophy of their skill at arms; it was the gift of victory from the Lord.

We sense in David's worship his humble gratitude to God for such dedicated men. At the same time, we see the renewing of David's faith. If God enabled three of his men to penetrate to the well of Bethlehem, surely God would deliver the Philistines into his hand and give him a full victory.

This beautiful story shows the sensitivity of David, his devotion to the Lord and to those through whom the Lord would bring victory. We read on through the chapter, and find that after the accounts of the exploits of David's mighty men, we have the honor roll of their names. At the end of the list we read: "Zelek the Ammonite, Naharai the Beerothite, the armor-bearer of Joab son of Zeruiah, Ira the Ithrite, Gareb the Ithrite and Uriah the Hittite. There were thirty-seven in all" (2 Sam. 23:37-39).

Reading that list, we come to the last of the names: Uriah the Hittite! He, too, was one of David's mighty men— as devoted to the king as the three who brought water from Bethlehem. The name of Uriah was stamped on the darkest chapter of the life of David. Later in David's reign, he remained in Jerusalem while his army was in the field besieging the Ammonite city of Rabbah (2 Sam. 11:1-27). At ease on the roof of his palace, David saw a woman bathing in a nearby garden. He was told that she was Bathsheba, the wife of one of his warriors, Uriah, who was fighting in the army. David had her brought to him, and took her to his bed. She returned home, and apparently David, having satisfied his lust, considered the affair at an end.

But Bathsheba sent word to David that she was pregnant. David devised a shameful strategy to make it appear that Uriah was the father of the child. He had his veteran campaigner brought home from the siege, confident that he would sleep with his wife. His scheme failed because of the devotion of Uriah to his comrades and his king. Uriah refused to go home; he was on duty, not on leave: "The ark and Israel and Judah are staying in tents, and my master Joab and my lord's men are camped in the open fields. How could I go to my house to eat and drink and lie with my wife?" (2 Sam. 11:11). After reporting the progress of the campaign to David, Uriah remained at the gate of the palace, sleeping with the soldiers of the guard.

The following evening David wined and dined him till he was drunk, but to no effect. When he saw that Uriah would not go home, David sent him back to his general Joab with a note that was his death warrant: "Put Uriah in the front line where the fighting is fiercest. Then withdraw from him so he will be struck down and die."

Devoted Uriah carried the king's message to his chief, and a few days later he was dead. David the adulterer had become David the murderer. He brought Bathsheba into his palace—at the price of Uriah's life.

Later, Nathan the prophet denounced David's crime. David sincerely repented of the evil he had done; Psalm 51 expresses the anguish of his heart. God forgave him, yet David had undermined his own authority in the life of his family. He eventually reaped what he had sown in the rebellion of his son Absalom.

David, like Samson, was a sinner. His place in the history of God's redemption is grounded in his calling, not in his obedience. Quite evidently, David is far from a perfect example for us. Yet David was a man of faith, who repented of sin and trusted in the Lord's salvation.

In his royal role, David points us to Jesus Christ, the Son of David, whom David called "Lord" (Ps. 110:1; Mt. 22:41-46; Acts 2:34-36). It is to King Jesus, not King David, that we bring the water of our spontaneous devotion. Jesus, indeed, looks for our devotion. When He healed ten lepers and only one returned to praise God at the feet of Jesus, the Lord asked, "Where are the other nine?" (Lk. 17:17). Since He had commanded them to show themselves to the priests, they could cover their ingratitude by claiming that they were doing exactly what Jesus had told them to do. After all, He had not said a word about returning to give thanks!

But true devotion is spontaneous. As in the case of David's warriors, devoted servants of the King do not wait to be asked. Indeed, devotion rejoices in surprises. To be sure, we cannot surprise the Lord of Glory—but we can try!

Jesus our King offers our devotion to the Father, for He is also our High Priest. In the sanctuary of heaven He offers as incense the prayers of the saints. The poor and imperfect ways in which we seek to glorify our Father are taken by our royal Mediator and presented as offerings well pleasing to God.

Jesus, who stands in David's place, is also our Warrior King. It is He who breaks through the enemy lines to bring to us the water of life. The water from Bethlehem was precious to David, for he saw it as "the blood of men that went at the risk of their lives." The cup that Jesus offers to us is brought, not simply at the risk of His life, but at the price of His life. It is the cup of the New Covenant in His blood.

The amazing grace of God appears in the devotion that He directs to us. The Old Testament term for loyalty or devotion (*chesed*) is used almost exclusively, not of our devotion toward God, but of His devotion toward us.[3] David, in his prayer of penitence after his fearful sin, dared to ask for God's mercy because of God's *chesed*: "Have mercy on me, O God, according to your unfailing love [*chesed*]" (Ps. 51:1).

Through the prophet, God says: "I have loved you with an everlasting love; I have drawn you with loving-kindness [*chesed*]" (Jer. 31:3).

The unfolding of God's plan of salvation reveals His *chesed* in the gift of His only begotten Son. Clearly it was God's faithfulness to David that carried His promise forward in spite of David's sin. The story of David recounts the past to point toward the future. God's choosing of David underlies the story of the book of Ruth. The book has its climax in the birth of Obed, the father of Jesse, David's father. It is a beautiful love story. Above all it shows the power of devotion. Naomi's devotion to the Lord was tested by the tragedies of her life. Exiled by the pressures of famine, Naomi lost her husband and her two sons. She returned empty to the land of her fathers. She was a widow, with no sons to claim the inheritance of the family or to continue the name of the family in Israel.

Yet she did not return alone. Her daughter-in-law Ruth refused to be separated from her. She clung to Naomi in devotion, claiming Naomi's land, people, and God as her own. She became the provider for the impoverished widow, gleaning in the fields of Bethlehem according to Naomi's instructions. God's faithful mercy guided Ruth to the lands of Boaz, who showed great kindness to the young stranger. Devotion now meets devotion. Ruth, who was better to Naomi than seven sons (Ruth 4:15), was willing to become the wife of Boaz, an older man, in order to secure for Naomi the inheritance of her family. Boaz, in turn, was willing to endanger his own estate in order to redeem the forfeited inheritance of Naomi, and to establish as his heir the son that Ruth would bear him.

Through all this lovely story of devotion within the covenant there shines the love of God and the devotion of His grace. Boaz was eligible to redeem the lands of Naomi's husband because he was a kinsman. The law of Moses specified the function of the *go'el*, the kinsman-redeemer (Lev. 25:25,48-49). But God Himself is the *Go'el* of the fatherless and the widow (Prov. 23:10-11). When Boaz met Ruth, he blessed her in the name of the Lord, the God of Israel, "under whose wings you have come to take refuge" (Ruth 2:12). Naomi, touched by the kindness of Boaz to Ruth, confessed, "The LORD . . . has not stopped showing his kindness [*chesed*] to the living and the dead" (Ruth 2:20). When little Obed was born to Ruth, the attending women said, "Praise be to the LORD, who this day has not left you without a kinsman-redeemer" (Ruth 4:14).

The story of Ruth paints the background for the narratives of King David. The line of the promise is continued. Obed is the son of Boaz, but because Boaz has redeemed the inheritance of Naomi, her friends put Obed in her lap and say with delight, "Naomi has a son" (Ruth 4:16). God's mercy leads the way to the birth of David by the faithfulness of a kinsman-redeemer. God's *chesed* to Naomi is one with His *chesed* to David. The purpose of God's mercy that leads to David leads also beyond David. His promise to David points to David's greater Son. Further, in the figure of Boaz, the redeeming grace of God is portrayed. God, who redeemed Israel from Egypt (Ex. 6:6), is the Kinsman-Redeemer. He procures the inheritance of His people as one bound to them with ties, as it were, of blood. The Lord, the Go'el of His people, will deliver them from their captivity (Jer. 50:34). Isaiah uses the terms for kinsman-redeemer to describe the coming salvation of the Lord (Is. 43:1,14; 44:22-23; 48:20; 52:3; 63:9,16).

The New Testament speaks of the costliness of the redemption price paid by the Father: it is the blood of His own Son (1 Pet. 1:18-19). At the same time, we are pointed to the work of Christ as our Redeemer. He has become our kinsman, made one flesh with us so that He might purchase for us the eternal inheritance of His salvation (Ro. 8:3,29).

The book of Ruth, then, gives the background for the calling of David, showing how the thread of God's promise was not broken. The line leading to David is important, not simply as royal genealogy, but as God's continuing work leading on to the ultimate fulfillment. At the same time, the figure of the kinsman-redeemer in Ruth points to the deep need that must be met by God's anointed.

God's people must be redeemed from more than poverty and oppression. David's own experience shows how deep that need is. He pleads for the *chesed* that the Lord had shown to his fathers; he needs deliverance, not only from his enemies but also from his transgressions (Ps. 39:8; 51:14; 109:21). David miserably failed in his devotion to those devoted to him. His hope was the faithful devotion of his God.

The story of David passes from the injuries and persecution he unjustly suffered in the earlier part of his life to the chastening of the Lord that marked the latter part. His sin with Bathsheba was forgiven in God's mercy; he did not lose his life or his crown. After the child of the adulterous union was taken away in God's judgment, Bathsheba bore David another son. David named him "Solomon," but the Lord named him "Jedidiah" ("Beloved of the LORD"—2 Sam. 12:25, NKJV). God's faithfulness did not desert David. The Lord did not revoke His promise that a Son of David's line would inherit an everlasting kingdom (2 Sam. 7:13).

Yet the solemn words of Nathan the prophet were fulfilled in the life of David. Listen to Nathan's indictment as he confronts David with his sin: "Now, therefore, the sword will never depart from your house, because you despised me and took the wife of Uriah the Hittite to be your own" (2 Sam. 12:10).

David's government of his own household was less wise than his government of Israel. He was by turns too lenient and too strict in dealing with incest and rebellion among his own children. The harvest of his sin and weakness was reaped in the rebellion of his son Absalom and the shocking violation of David's wives by Absalom when he drove his father from Jerusalem. David, fleeing for his life with his faithful men, was cursed and mocked by Shimei, an old enemy from the house of Saul. Shimei followed David's band, casting stones and insults. Abishai, one of David's generals, offered to silence Shimei: "Why should this dead dog curse my lord the king? Let me go over and cut off his head" (2 Sam. 16:9).

David rebuked the bitter vengefulness of Abishai. "My son, who is of my own flesh, is trying to take my life. How much more, then, this Benjamite!" David accepted the humiliation as from God's hand. "It may be that the LORD will see my distress and repay me with good for the cursing I am receiving today."

In the depth of his humiliation, David looked to the

Lord to deliver and vindicate him. His faith held fast to God. At the same time, David, though unjustly attacked and persecuted, was far from innocent himself. Chastised by the Lord, he was restored to his throne and could preside over the enthronement of his son Solomon, God's chosen successor.

On the one hand, David was a man after God's own heart, the king whose devotion to the Lord led all Israel in worship. On the other hand, David's great sin showed the imperfection of his devotion. Both sides of David's life were reflected in God's promise to him. As the devoted servant of the Lord, King David desired to build a house of God in Jerusalem, the place where God would set His name and dwell among His people. Because David desired to build God's house, God promised to build David's house: to establish his kingdom forever (2 Sam. 7:11,16).

But because David himself did not measure up to the ideal of God's anointed, God's promise was directed to a future Son of David (2 Sam. 7:12-13). Initially, God's promise pointed to Solomon, who would build the Temple in Jerusalem using the resources provided by David. But as David himself recognized, the promised Son would be far greater than Solomon: "The LORD says to my Lord: 'Sit at my right hand until I make your enemies a footstool for your feet'" (Ps. 110:1).

David's faith in the Lord not only embraced the promise but strained forward in hope, longing for fulfillment in a Son who would be his Lord, seated on a heavenly throne and given universal dominion.

The story of David in the Old Testament provides the foundation for our understanding of the Psalms. David himself was a psalmist par excellence. From his early youth he played the harp in the sheep fields. As king, he was still the "sweet psalmist" of Israel (2 Sam. 23:1). In addition to the

Psalms that he wrote, he provided for composers and singers to lead the praises of Israel. David's Psalms and the other inspired songs of Israel carry forward the story of Jesus.

This is particularly plain in the Psalms that we recognize as Messianic. Psalm 22, for example, begins with the cry that came from the lips of Jesus on the cross: "My God, my God, why have you forsaken me?" The Psalm describes in graphic detail the agony of the Crucified ("All my bones are out of joint. . . . They have pierced my hands and my feet"), and the mocking of His enemies ("All who see me mock me; they hurl insults, shaking their heads: he trusts in the LORD; let the LORD rescue him. . . . They divide my garments among them and cast lots for my clothing"). We know of no time in the life of David when he was so tortured and shamed. In this Psalm he describes his sufferings in vivid language that was figurative hyperbole for his experience, but was literal in a startling way when his inspired words were fulfilled at Calvary.

It is not only in Psalms that so specifically refer to Christ that we are pointed forward to Him. When we examine Psalm 22, for example, we notice that it is similar to many other Psalms.[4] It has the form of a lament, the lament of an individual. This is the commonest form found in the Psalter. (There are "we" Psalms, such as Psalm 100, as well as "I" psalms, such as Psalm 22.) Psalm 22 begins with the cry of abandonment, a cry that turns to lament:

> O my God, I cry out by day, but you do not answer,
>   by night, and am not silent.

This plaint is followed by a confession of trust:

> Yet you are enthroned as the Holy One;
>   you are the praise of Israel.

In you our fathers put their trust;
    they trusted and you delivered them.
They cried to you and were saved;
    in you they trusted and were not disappointed.

After these words of trust, David turns again to lamenting his condition: "I am a worm and not a man, scorned by men and despised by the people." He describes the bitter mockery of his enemies, then again remembers God's faithfulness.

Yet you brought me out of the womb;
    you made me trust in you even at my mother's
        breast.
From birth I was cast upon you;
    from my mother's womb you have been my God.

The alternating descriptions of distress and of trust lead to a cry for deliverance:

Do not be far from me,
    for trouble is near and there is no one to help.

Again the psalmist turns to describing the agony of his situation. He tells of the ferocity of his foes. They are like wild bulls, roaring lions, snarling dogs. In contrast, he is stripped and defenseless, his strength gone; he is transfixed and perishing. A constant triad appears in the lament: they, I, and you. *They*, my enemies, are murderous; *I* am helpless; *You*, Lord, have forsaken me. In this desperate situation, the suffering servant of the Lord can only cry from the depths to the heights:

But you, O LORD, be not far off;
    O my Strength, come quickly to help me.

Deliver my life from the sword,
    my precious life from the power of the dogs.
Rescue me from the mouth of the lions;
    save me from the horns of the wild oxen.

Will the cry of the Lord's abandoned servant be heard? Yes! After the cry for salvation, David bursts into a vow of praise:

I will declare your name to my brothers;
    in the congregation I will praise you.

The praise of God in the midst of the congregation is a reference to the thank offering (Lev. 7:11-18). In deep distress a worshiper would pray to God for deliverance and vow to bring an offering of praise when the prayer was heard. Although the psalmist is still in the anguish of his suffering, he speaks with confidence of the offering of praise that he will bring to the Lord when his deliverance comes. With that salvation in view, David closes the Psalm with a magnificent doxology, ending in a shout of praise: "He has done it!"

David by inspiration goes far beyond his own experience. He anticipates the suffering and deliverance of the One who is to come, his Son and Lord. The author of Hebrews recognizes this, for he attributes to Christ the vow of praise from the Psalm:

In bringing many sons to glory, it was fitting that God, for whom and through whom everything exists, should make the author of their salvation perfect through suffering. . . . So Jesus is not ashamed to call them brothers. He says, "I will declare your name to my brothers; in the presence of the congregation I will sing your praises." (Heb. 2:10-12)

Not only does Jesus own the cry of abandonment at the opening of the psalm; the vow of praise is also His. Jesus is a singing Savior, leading the praises of the redeemed. Paul describes Christ as singing among the Gentiles a song of praise. In Romans, the apostle to the Gentiles declares:

> For I say that Christ hath been made a minister of the circumcision for the truth of God, that he might confirm the promises *given* unto the fathers, and that the Gentiles might glorify God for his mercy; as it is written, "Therefore will I give praise unto thee among the Gentiles, and sing unto thy name." (Ro. 15:8-9, ASV)

Paul's quotation is from Psalm 18:49. Who is the "I" in the passage as he cites it? Clearly it is Christ. Paul says that Christ has been made a minister of the circumcision—not in the sense that He ministers *to* the circumcision, but that He ministers *for* the circumcision.[5] Christ is Himself circumcised, and He fulfills the calling of the circumcision so as to confirm the promises given to the fathers. God promised Abraham that in him all the families of the earth would be blessed. Circumcision was the seal of that promise of God. Jesus Christ fulfilled God's covenant with Abraham and with Israel. He inherited all the promises of God, and He proclaims the victory of God's salvation to the Gentiles.

In Psalm 18, David pictures his vow of thankful praise being offered to God not merely before God's people but before all nations. He thinks of God's house as established in the midst of the earth so that God's presence might be made known to all peoples. David's own deliverance bears witness to God's power and grace, so that all the world might know. David wrote this Psalm to pray for deliverance from Saul, yet his inspired communion with God caught the deeper meaning of his victory as God's anointed: "Great deliverance giveth he to his king; and showeth mercy to his anointed, to David, and to his seed for evermore" (Ps. 18:50, KJV).

Paul recognized that God's deliverance was given at last to the Seed of David, the true King of the nations (Gal. 3:16). He therefore pictured Christ as singing the praises of the Father in a missionary hymn of gospel triumph.

Paul's use of Psalm 18 in reference to Christ helps us to recognize that it is not only in the clearly Messianic Psalms that Christ is to be seen. The Psalms are celebrations of God's covenant with His people. They claim God's promise to be the God of His people. The psalmist, either David or another, speaks to the Lord of the covenant as His servant.[6] Since Christ is the Lord of the covenant who comes as the Servant of the covenant, the Psalms center on Him in whom the covenant is fulfilled. Not only are there numerous Psalms that have the form of Psalm 22; the elements of that Psalm are often found in separate Psalms of trust, assurance, praise for being heard, or doxology. Psalm 23, for example, is a Psalm of trust.

There are Psalms of other kinds; they, too, point us to Christ, as the New Testament shows. We are accustomed to seeing Christ revealed as the Lord our Shepherd in Psalm 23 (Jn. 10). He is no less the Lord of all the Psalms, our Creator and Redeemer (Is. 43:15; Ps. 102:25-28; Heb. 1:10-12; Ps. 68:18; Eph. 4:8), who walks on the waves of the sea to deliver His own (Ps. 77:19; Job 9:8; Mt. 14:25,33).

Christ, David's greater Son, is the Servant of the royal Psalms (Ps. 45:6-7; Heb. 1:8-9; Ps. 2:7; Heb. 1:5; Ps. 110:1; Mt. 22:4-6; Ps. 118:26; Mt. 21:9). He is the second Adam, the Head of a new humanity (Ps. 8:4-6; Heb. 2:6-9). He is both the Righteous Servant who ascends into the hill of the Lord, and the Lord of Glory, to whom the everlasting gates are opened (Ps. 24). The wisdom Psalms point to Him who is our Wisdom (1 Cor. 1:24,30).

NOTES:
1. Another play on words: the place is called "Ramath Lehi," the "Heights of Lehi." *Ramath*, however, is also related to the verb for "throw," as though the hill took its name from the throwing of the jawbone (expressed by another verb). The name of the spring is "the spring of the one who calls," applicable to Samson's cry, although the term describes the partridge as a "caller" bird ("the spring of the partridge").
2. Psalm 110:6-7—I have changed the NKJV translation "dead bodies" to "bodies." The word does not mean only corpses. "Dead bodies" is a fair translation in the context of the Psalm, but Paul's allusion picks up on the word and gives another meaning to "bodies." I have also omitted "the places" in verse 6, since the more literal translation makes Paul's use of the vocabulary clearer.
3. See Francis I. Andersen, "Yahweh, the Kind and Sensitive God" in P.T. O'Brien & D.G. Peterson, eds., *God Who Is Rich in Mercy* (Grand Rapids: Baker Book House, 1986), pages 41-88.
4. On the literary form of the Psalms, see Robert Alter, *The Art of Biblical Poetry* (New York: Basic Books Inc., 1985).
5. The NIV translation of Romans 15:8, ". . . that Christ has become a servant of the Jews," obscures the point Paul is making.
6. See the superscription to Psalm 36: "Of David the servant of the LORD."

8

THE PRINCE OF PEACE

David, the Lord's anointed, celebrated the promise God gave him of the Messianic King to come (Ps. 110). The glory of God's covenant with David remains a theme of the praises of Israel (Ps. 89; 132). That promise continued to be remembered by the prophets before the exile (Amos 9:11; Mic. 5:1-5; Is. 9:5-6), on the eve of the exile (Jer. 23:5-6; 30:9), during the exile (Ezk. 34:23-24; 37:21-25), and after the exile (Zech. 12:8).[1] God's promise of the Messiah to come was given to David when he had determined to build a Temple to the Lord. God denied his request. David would not build God's house; rather, God would build David's house. He would establish his Son's throne forever (2 Sam. 7:11,16). David was not called to build the Temple, for he was a warrior, a man who had shed blood in battle (1 Chron. 28:3). When the wars of David were over, when the Lord had subdued all the enemies of his kingdom; then, and only then, would the Temple be built (1 Ki. 5:3).

The reign of Solomon completes the reign of David. In the ancient Near East, the culmination of a king's military campaigns was often commemorated by the building of a palace or a temple. David won the victories on which Solomon's peaceful reign was established. He prepared for the Temple by gathering a great store of materials for its construction (1 Ki. 7:51; 1 Chron. 22:2-5).

The two reigns must therefore be taken together; together, David and Solomon picture the Lord's king. David, the royal warrior, is succeeded by Solomon, the prince of peace ("Solomon," from *shalom*, means "peaceful"—see 1 Chron. 22:9). While Solomon is not the Son of David in whom all the promises are fulfilled, he does stand as a type of Christ, the Prince of Peace. The royal Psalms idealize the reign of Solomon, using it as a model to point forward to the true and final King (Ps. 2; 45; 72).

David's sufferings, so vividly expressed in his psalms, mark him as the suffering servant of the Lord. Saul hated and pursued him without any cause (Ps. 35:19; 69:4). He was betrayed by one closest to him (Ahithophel, his friend and counselor—2 Sam. 15:12): "Even my close friend, whom I trusted, he who shared my bread, has lifted up his heel against me" (Ps. 41:9).

The Gospel of John calls our attention to the way in which David's sufferings point to Christ's (Jn. 13:18; 15:25). Even the geographical details have vivid similarities. David, too, left Jerusalem and crossed the Kidron to the slope of the Mount of Olives.

In the midst of his sufferings and humiliation, David constantly showed mercy toward his enemies, so much so that his general Joab accused him of loving those who hated him (2 Sam. 19:6). On one occasion, in his outlaw days, he was about to use his sword to exact tribute and bring vengeance on Nabal, whose flocks he had been protecting

(1 Sam. 25:9-13). But he heeded the plea of Abigail, Nabal's wife, when she met him to intercept his raid. He praised God for deterring him from executing his own vengeance. The Lord avenged Nabal's folly.

On the other hand, David did charge Solomon with the execution of swift justice against those who had hated and betrayed him (1 Ki. 2:2-9), a commission that Solomon fulfilled. This action on David's part need not be seen as a weakness in his character, as though he shrank from the consequences of administering justice. We may, indeed, feel that David was weak at times in dealing with transgression and crime. But David's charge to Solomon takes account of the difference in their reigns. David bears not only the agony of battle, but also the reproach of those who betrayed and disobeyed him. Solomon brings in the kingdom in which peace is founded on stern justice.

David foreshadows the longsuffering restraint of Christ's humiliation. Solomon typifies Christ as the Judge, who ushers in the Kingdom by judging justly. Christ's rule as the Prince of Peace is grounded in the perfect justice of His judgment. The fulfillment is, of course, far richer than the foreshadowing. We cannot simply take King David to be the type of Christ's first coming and King Solomon of His second coming.

On the one hand, Christ's kingdom rule was evident even in the days of His suffering: the demons obeyed Him. On the other hand, the justice that He will bring with Him when He comes again is the justice of the Lamb on the throne. The glory of Christ's rule is not still future; it is already established in heaven. Jesus not only goes to prepare a place for us; He has already built the new Temple by His resurrection and by the union of His people to Himself. Nevertheless, the marked contrast between David and Solomon helps us recognize the contrast between the humiliation and exaltation of Christ: His longsuffering grace and His final justice.

Solomon's reign brought the history of the people of God to a mountaintop. The craftsmen had put the finishing touches on the carved cedar and wrought gold of the Temple; Huram of Tyre had cast bronze into huge pillars and delicate capitals, basins, shovels, and sprinkling bowls. Seven years of construction had converted an immense treasury into the glory of a Temple without rival.

Solomon assembled all the elders and leaders of Israel to dedicate the house of God, the place on earth where the Lord would set His name, where His glory would dwell. Hundreds of priests offered uncounted numbers of sheep and cattle. The priests and Levites bore the ark of the Lord into the holy of holies; the cloud of God's presence filled His house with glory and His people's hearts with awe. The long march of the centuries had come to rest. God had brought His people from the darkness of Egyptian bondage to the lightning of Sinai and then to Mount Zion, the place of His dwelling in the midst of His inheritance.

Solomon stood before the people and praised God for keeping all His promises: not only His promise to David that his son would build the Temple, but His promises to Moses as well. "Praise be to the LORD, who has given rest to his people Israel just as he promised. Not one word has failed of all the good promises he gave through his servant Moses" (1 Ki. 8:56).

It is in this setting of the fulfillment of the promises of God that the theme of wisdom comes to the fore. Solomon, offered his choice of the blessings of God, asked for wisdom, and his request was abundantly granted (1 Ki. 3:4-15). Indeed, the wisdom that God gave to Solomon became the blessing that fulfilled God's promise, not just to Moses but to Abraham. In the seed of Abraham all the nations of the earth would be blessed. When Israel was established in the land and the house of God set up, the time had come for blessing to flow out to the nations. This happened in the reign of Solomon.

> God gave Solomon wisdom and very great insight, and a breadth of understanding as measureless as the sand on the seashore. . . . And his fame spread to all the surrounding nations. He spoke three thousand proverbs and his songs numbered a thousand and five. He described plant life, from the cedar of Lebanon to the hyssop that grows out of walls. He also taught about animals and birds, reptiles and fish. Men of all nations came to listen to Solomon's wisdom, sent by all the kings of the world, who had heard of his wisdom. (1 Ki. 4:29-34)

The visit of the queen of Sheba to hear the wisdom of Solomon has been so shaped by the Hollywood version that we have forgotten its place in the history of redemption. Not only did royalty send ambassadors to the court of Solomon. In the case of Sheba, the queen herself came to discover the truth of the reports she had heard. She was overwhelmed: the half had not been told her. How fortunate were the servants of the king, to have the privilege of standing before him and hearing the wisdom of his judgments! (1 Ki. 10:8). The queen blessed the God of Israel: "Because of the LORD's eternal love for Israel, he has made you king, to maintain justice and righteousness" (1 Ki. 10:9).

The nations were drawn not simply by Israel, prospering under God's blessing, but by the king of Israel, who was given encyclopedic wisdom. Solomon's wisdom was compared with that of the wise men of the ancient world: he exceeds them all. The ideal of wisdom includes comprehen-

sive inquiry into the world of creation. But Solomon dili-
gently pursued biology as well as statecraft and literature. His
wisdom was not parochial but international, cosmopolitan.
Yet there would come a humble King who could quietly
declare, "One greater than Solomon is here" (Mt. 12:42).

In the proverbs of Solomon no less than in the psalms of
David, we are pointed toward Jesus Christ. The golden text
of the book of Proverbs is: "The fear of the LORD is the
beginning of wisdom, and knowledge of the Holy One is
understanding" (Prov. 9:10). Apart from the Lord, the
acquisition of knowledge is meaningless. The ultimate and
supreme reality is not fire or water, as early Greek philosophy imagined, nor is it an abstract set of ideas. It is not
"Being." It is the living God, who revealed Himself to Israel,
and summoned the nations of the earth to heed His word.
We are prepared to learn that the Logos is not an abstract
principle, but the Son of the Father.

God is the Possessor of wisdom (Prov. 3:19). Indeed, in
a remarkable figure, God's wisdom is personified as His
companion, present with Him in the creation of the world
(Prov. 8:22). God's wisdom is revealed in His works: the
created world and the course of nature and history (Prov.
8:22-31; Ps. 33:6-21). God expresses His wisdom in His
word. His word not only controls all things, but is spoken to
His people so that they might know the Lord (Ps. 147:18-19).

Knowing and fearing the Lord is therefore the beginning
of all of our thinking, the realistic thinking that will direct
our lives (Prov. 3:5,7; 12:15). Wisdom is not just information storage and retrieval; it is informed awareness of who we
are and before whom we stand. By calling us to make God the
Lord of our knowing as well as our living, the wisdom
literature directs us toward the personal revelation of God in
Jesus Christ. On the other hand, the wisdom books and
psalms of the Old Testament also prepare for Christ in a

negative way: "'Meaningless! Meaningless!' says the Teacher. 'Utterly meaningless! Everything is meaningless'" (Eccl. 1:2).

The despair expressed in the book of Ecclesiastes has a particular place in the history of God's saving work. The promises of God have been kept. The people of God now live in their land; they have not only their daily bread but milk and honey besides. A man may enjoy the shade of his own fig tree while the sun shines on his grapevines. The inheritance the people of Israel had longed for and fought for has been acquired. It is time to reflect. Beer commercials on American television have pictured a group of friends sitting on the porch of a lodge after a day of fishing. The sun is setting, and they are sharing a couple of six-packs. "It doesn't get any better than this," says one of them.

The commercial raises a disturbing question, even for a fisherman who might regard an evening beer as life's crowning pleasure. Life might not get any better, but it will certainly get worse. Life itself moves toward a sunset, if it doesn't crash sooner. What meaning does life have that is not canceled by death? Many a six-pack has been emptied in an effort to postpone that question, but the question will not go away.

If the average Israelite under his fig tree is not asking the question, then the wise man is. Even though the blessings of peace and abundance have been given to Israel, can this be all that there is? The working man labors all his life, but what does he have to show for it at last? He must leave behind all that he worked for (Eccl. 5:15). The wise man may be just as diligent in honing his understanding, but at last he dies like the fool (Eccl. 2:16). The cycles of life slide by, but what meaning can they have?

The "Preacher" of Ecclesiastes does, indeed, point to the only possible resolution of the enigmas of life. The key is to be found with God. This philosophic author of Ecclesiastes contrasts the emptiness of human labor with the hidden work of God (Eccl. 8:17; 11:5). He confesses that the wisdom of God is unfathomable, and counsels men to fear God and keep His commandments, trusting Him for what they cannot understand (12:13-14). Yet the sober faith of this answer points powerfully to a fuller answer to come, an answer that is unfolded in the prophets. There is more to come: a greater rest than rest from Philistine invaders, a greater peace than Solomon could provide, a greater inheritance than the land of promise. There is more to come, because God is to come. When He comes, death the devourer will be devoured in victory (Is. 25:8; 1 Cor. 15:54-56). Suffering as well as death is a problem confronted in the wisdom sections of the Old Testament. David's cry to the Lord in the laments of his Psalms leads us to the promise of God's deliverance. The book of Job faces the mystery of the suffering of the righteous. The easy answers of Job's comforters are set aside, but at last Job must bow before God's sovereignty and look for the resolution that can come only from Him. Not only do the righteous suffer while the wicked seem to prosper. Evil nations, too, drive the helpless before them, as the dragnet of their military power sweeps across the earth. Jeremiah laments not only his own condition but also the desolation of the people of God.

Daniel the prophet was also a sage. His visions offered the answer of divine wisdom to the temporary triumph of pagan world empires. God's own Kingdom would come as a stone cut without hands, striking the image of imperial power and demolishing it. At last, only the Kingdom of God would cover the earth, as the waters cover the sea.

Jesus comes as the Son of David, the divine Warrior, to overcome the hosts of darkness. He comes also as the One greater than Solomon. He is the Prince of Peace who is the very Wisdom of God. Matthew's Gospel tells us how Jesus rejoiced in the wisdom of His Father: "I praise you, Father, Lord of heaven and earth, because you have hidden these things from the wise and learned, and revealed them to little children. Yes, Father, for this was your good pleasure" (Mt. 11:25-26). Jesus calls the weary and burdened to come to Him and to take His yoke of wisdom: "Come to me, all you who are weary and burdened, and I will give you rest. Take my yoke upon you and learn from me, for I am gentle and humble in heart, and you will find rest for your souls. For my yoke is easy and my burden is light" (Mt. 11:28-30).

Jesus here uses the language of wisdom. There is a strikingly similar passage to be found in the *Wisdom of the Son of Sirach* (*Ecclesiasticus*):

> Turn in unto me, ye unlearned, and lodge in my house of instruction. How long will ye lack these things? And how long shall your soul be so athirst? I open my mouth and speak of her. Acquire Wisdom for yourselves without money. Bring your necks under her yoke, and her burden let your soul bear; she is nigh unto them that seek her, and he that is intent (upon her) findeth her. Behold with your eyes that I have laboured but little therein, and abundance of peace have I found. (Ecclesiasticus 51:23-27)[2]

As in the wisdom passage, Jesus issues a summons, calls on His hearers to come, take the yoke and learn. The son of Sirach promises much rest with little labor. Jesus, too, promises rest and says that His burden is light. Yet there is an amazing difference. Jesus does not call us to take the yoke of wisdom, but to take *His* yoke. He speaks not just as a teacher of wisdom, but as the Lord of wisdom. He calls us to learn, not of wisdom in the abstract but of Him in Person. As Lord,

He steps into the role of wisdom and calls us to Himself.

The basis for the astonishing claim of Jesus is given in the preceding verse of Matthew's Gospel: "All things have been committed to me by my Father. No one knows the Son except the Father, and no one knows the Father except the Son and those to whom the Son chooses to reveal him" (Mt. 11:27).

Jesus, the eternal Son of the Father, claims exclusive knowledge of God. There is a sense in which any son knows his father in a unique way; this human relation provides a faint analogy of what is true of the divine Trinity. Apart from the revelation of the Son, who is the eternal Image of the Father (Col. 1:15; 2:9; Jn. 1:18), there can be no knowledge of Him. Since God the Son is no less divine than the Father, it is also true that the Son can be known only as the Father wills (Jn. 6:44). True wisdom is not the achievement of man's effort; it is the gift of God's grace. Neither scientific research nor muttered mantras will disclose the truth that gives meaning to our lives. Truth at last is personal: "I am the way and the truth and the life. No one comes to the Father except through me" (Jn. 14:6).

The gospel that the New Testament proclaims calls us to Jesus Christ as the Wisdom of God. The personification of wisdom in Proverbs 8 foreshadowed the revelation of a deeper reality. Wisdom is not just an attribute of God that may be pictured poetically as serving God in His work of creation. Wisdom is personal in the being of the Son of God.

The Gospel of John begins with the affirmation that the Word of God is personal, God's companion and eternal Son, true God who became man. By calling the divine Son the Word (*Logos*), John was ascribing to Him the role of Wisdom, a theme much pursued in Jewish reflection on the Old Testament. (He was also presenting a perspective of the Son over against the *Logos* in Greek philosophy.)

The same connection is made by the apostle Paul in Colossians. He speaks of Christ as the Image of the invisible God, the One through whom God is revealed, and in whom the "fullness," the totality of God's being, resides (Col. 1:15,19; 2:9). In the *Wisdom of Solomon*, an apocryphal book written before the birth of Christ, wisdom is described as an "effulgence from everlasting light" and an image of God's goodness (Wisd. 7:26).

When Paul describes the Son of God as the Agent of creation and the Image of God, he is attributing to Christ the place of divine Wisdom. Indeed, he is doing more, for he declares that the One whose glory he saw on the road to Damascus is the One for whom all things were created, and in whom all things hold together, the very person of God in bodily form (Col. 2:9). The apostle bore witness to the truth of the claim of Jesus: He is the Wisdom of God.

The majesty of Christ's claim in Matthew 11:27-30 is no more awesome than its grace. Jesus calls men to learn of Him who is meek and lowly in heart. The mighty Lord of wisdom bows His own neck to bear the yoke of His Father's word, and the cross of His Father's will. The cross is foolishness to the wisdom of this world, but it is the wisdom of God for our salvation. At Calvary, Jesus Christ is made to be for us wisdom, righteousness, holiness, and redemption (1 Cor. 1:18-31).

In Christ, God's answer is given to the enigmas that baffled the wisdom of Solomon. Death is swallowed up in victory, because Christ has drawn the sting of death by paying the price of sin. He has destroyed the grip of death in the power of His resurrection. The mystery of the suffering of righteous people is transformed by His suffering, who is the Holy One of God. He suffered for us, leaving us an example, that we should follow in His steps (1 Pet. 2:21). Suffering now becomes for us the privilege of fellowship with Jesus. Secular kingdoms may rise and fall, but the Kingdom of Christ has been established. He is already at the right hand of God and will come again to judge and to establish God's righteousness forever in a new heavens and earth.

Through the Word and the Spirit of Christ, His disciples grow in true wisdom. The richly indwelling Word of Christ illumines our understanding as we address one another in psalms, hymns, and spiritual songs, singing with grace in our hearts to God (Col. 3:16). We grow in wisdom as we prove out in our lives the things that are pleasing to God.

The Lord has withdrawn the Urim and the Thummim, the mysterious objects in the ephod of the high priest that enabled David to secure "yes" or "no" answers from God (1 Sam. 23:2,9). Children must be guided by such answers. But when they come of age, they learn to understand something of the mind of their parents. So, too, the Lord wants us to grow in wisdom, coming to understand the mind of Christ. We cannot secure a blueprint of our lives in advance. Wisdom grows right in the situation; thus we prayerfully prove out the application of the word of God. In this situation and before this opportunity, we discern what is most pleasing to God. If the least in Christ's Kingdom is greater than John the Baptist, then the believer, filled with the Spirit of Christ, instructed by His word, and in fellowship with Him, may also have wisdom that exceeds that of Solomon.

Solomon's wisdom, indeed, failed him, for he neglected his own teaching. He began to rely on his own wisdom rather than on the Lord, whose fear is the beginning of wisdom. Since his was a small kingdom wedged between superpowers and since he was a man of peace, not of war, it seemed prudent to him to find his defense in peace treaties. What better way of sealing a treaty than by marrying a daughter of the king whose armies could prove a threat? Disregarding the law of God, Solomon married scores of heathen wives, for reasons of policy as well as pleasure. His actions were in direct contradiction to God's word through Moses, which warned the people not to make treaties with the heathen or to marry their daughters (Ex. 34:10-17).

Solomon dedicated God's Temple while the cloud of glory filled the sanctuary. But that same Solomon, later in his reign, stood on the Mount of Olives with his back to the glistening gold of God's Temple to choose a site for a shrine to Chemosh, the god of Moab (1 Ki. 11:7). Solomon, in all his wisdom, forgot that the Lord is a jealous God, who will not share His glory with an idol (Ex. 34:14).

God's judgment was pronounced against Solomon. The zenith of blessing had been reached. Now, through the idolatrous disobedience of Solomon, the long trail downward to the nadir of captivity began. A greater than Solomon was needed to bring righteousness and justice to the people of God.

NOTES:
1. Yves M.J. Congar has compared David and Solomon as types of Christ: "David et Salomon, Types du Christ en ses Deux Avénements" in *Les Voies du Dieu Vivant* (Paris: du Cerf, 1964), pages 149-164. I am indebted to his insights, although I disagree with the place he gives to good works in salvation.
2. R.H. Charles translation, *The Apocrypha and Pseudepigrapha of the Old Testament in English* (Oxford, England: Clarendon, 1913).

9

THE LORD TO COME

The Lord Must Come

After the days of Solomon, the history of Israel was a story of increasing apostasy and judgment. Solomon's kingdom was divided when his son Rehoboam met a tax protest with royal arrogance rather than wisdom. Under Jeroboam the ten northern tribes broke away from the throne of David. To solidify the independence of northern Israel, Jeroboam set up a new and idolatrous form of worship. So that Israelites would not continue to worship at Jerusalem, he erected golden calves at Dan and Bethel, near the northern and southern boundaries of his kingdom (1 Ki. 12:28-30). "Here are your gods, O Israel," he declared, "who brought you up out of Egypt." His words were an ominous repetition of the inauguration of calf worship at the foot of Mount Sinai.

Jeroboam established all the forms and institutions of apostate worship: priests, feast days, sacrifices, a cultus of human invention imitating but subverting the ordinances of the Lord. Worship at hilltop shrines was authorized; the Canaanite forms of religion that had always been a temptation to the people of God received official recognition. In the prophetic record of the history of Israel, God's sentence against the sin of Jeroboam is repeated again and again. It tolls against every later king who followed the practices of Jeroboam's apostasy: "He did evil in the eyes of the LORD, walking in the ways of Jeroboam and in his sin, which he caused Israel to commit" (1 Ki. 15:34).

Yet the Lord did not utterly cast off Israel. He sent prophets to them, beginning in the days of Jeroboam. They called Israel to repentance, pronounced God's judgments, and promised His forgiveness to those who would repent. Their messages were steadfastly ignored. The prophet Jeremiah spoke of twenty-three years of ministry with no response, and added: "And though the LORD has sent all his servants the prophets to you again and again, you have not listened or paid any attention" (Jer. 25:4).

At one point, Israel's apostasy took an even more virulent form. Jezebel, the heathen queen of King Ahab, succeeded in making the worship of the Tyrian god Baal the official royal cultus in Israel. Her success led Israel to take a last fatal step in religious apostasy. They moved from idolatry in the worship of the Lord to the worship of another god.

To break the grip of this popular heathenism, the Lord sent the judgment of drought. The drought was announced by God's prophet Elijah, who declared to Ahab, "As the LORD, the God of Israel, lives, whom I serve, there will be neither dew nor rain in the next few years except at my word" (1 Ki. 17:1).

As the seasons passed without rain, famine gripped Israel, and King Ahab mounted an international search for Elijah. The Lord had given Elijah refuge and ministry with a widow in Zarephath, a Gentile city near Sidon. Again the word of the Lord came to Elijah; he made a dramatic reappearance in Israel. Once more he confronted Ahab, and demanded a power encounter between the priests of Baal and himself as the sole prophet of the Lord. Let the true God show His power by giving rain to Israel!

Mount Carmel was the scene of the contest. King Ahab gathered the hundreds of prophets who served Baal and Asherah, the fertility god and goddess whose worship Ahab had sponsored. Thousands of Israelites covered the slopes of the mountain to witness the encounter. Since rain brought fertility, and fertility was the specialty of Baal and Asherah, the people must have expected them to produce. Elijah gave the prophets of Baal every advantage in the contest. Let them offer the first sacrifice, but let Baal provide the fire to show his acceptance of the bull they offered. Baal was a storm-god; let him ignite the wood with a bolt of lightning, and follow that with rain.

The prophets of Baal began to invoke their deity, but with no success. They produced a dramatic spectacle, but no fire or rain. By the hundreds they chanted, danced, and prophesied Baal's response. After hours of this, Elijah began to taunt them. "Shout louder!" he said. "Surely he is a god! Perhaps he is deep in thought, or busy, or traveling. Maybe he is sleeping and must be awakened" (1 Ki. 18:27).[1]

Spurred on by Elijah's ridicule, the prophets of Baal worked themselves into a frenzy, slashing themselves with swords and crying out to Baal. Not until evening and the time of the evening sacrifice did Elijah call a halt and rebuild the altar of the Lord. Twelve stones he used for the twelve tribes of Israel (not the ten tribes of Ahab's kingdom). He dug a trench around the altar and laid the sacrifice in order on the wood. He then commanded that the sacrifice and the altar be drenched with water. It was poured on until the trench was full. Elijah then prayed to Yahweh, the God of Abraham, Isaac, and Jacob: "Answer me, O LORD, answer me, so these people will know that you, O LORD, are God, and that you are turning their hearts back again" (1 Ki. 18:37).

The fire of the Lord fell. It consumed not only the wet wood and the sacrifice, but the stones, the water, and the very earth beneath the altar. The terrified crowd fell prostrate and cried, "The LORD—he is God! The LORD—he is God!"

In our skeptical age, many people demand just such a demonstration of the existence of the living God. Let God show by an atomic blast that He is Lord, that He can make or unmake at His word. That demand was made of Jesus. Ignoring the miracles that Jesus did, hostile skeptics demanded that He perform one more to order. Jesus refused.

God can, when He chooses, make His power known as He did at Mount Carmel. But the Almighty does not produce His credentials on demand for our inspection. For rebellious sinners to demand fire from heaven is the height of folly!

Yet if fire from heaven is too much, far more than we had bargained for, there is also a sense in which it is too little. God's fire from heaven could consume sinners as it consumed Sodom and Gomorrah. But fire from heaven cannot save sinners; it cannot accomplish the mystery of God's plan.

Elijah had to be taught that lesson. After the victory on Mount Carmel, Elijah was able to order the execution of God's sentence against the prophets of Baal. God sent the rain in torrents. It would seem that Elijah's triumph was complete, that he had restored the hearts of children to their fathers and the hearts of fathers to the God of Israel. But we learn that Queen Jezebel, furious at the execution of the prophets of Baal, vowed to kill Elijah. The prophet had to flee.

Alone and exhausted in the desert of the Arabah, exiled

Elijah despaired of his life. What victory was it on Carmel that left Ahab as king and Jezebel as queen? Who, indeed, remained to proclaim the word of the Lord but Elijah, and now his life was again in jeopardy. Elijah flung himself down under a broom tree. "I have had enough, LORD," he said. "Take my life; I am no better than my ancestors" (1 Ki. 19:4).

The Lord proceeded to instruct His demoralized prophet. He refreshed Elijah with sleep and food, and guided him to Horeb, the mountain of God in Sinai. When Elijah voiced his complaint, "I am the only one left," the Lord revealed His glory to Elijah, as He had once done to Moses on Mount Sinai. Elijah took shelter in a cave as a wind exceeding hurricane force tore apart the very rocks of the mountain. An earthquake shook the mountain. Fire fell on Mount Horeb as it had fallen on Mount Carmel. Yet, we are told, the Lord Himself was not present in any of these repercussions of almighty power. After the fire, however, Elijah heard a gentle whisper. He covered his face with his cloak and went out of the cave to meet with the Lord.

God's control of the world and of history do not require fire from heaven. It is enough for Him to speak for His will to be done. His word is sovereign and almighty; His purposes do not fail. The Lord spoke to Elijah, commanding him to anoint three individuals who would be, in different ways, God's instruments in the overthrow of Baalism in Israel. Hazael was to be anointed king of Syria; Jehu, king of Israel; and Elisha, God's prophet to succeed Elijah. A Gentile invader, a violent usurper, and a faithful minister of God's word would all be used in God's own time and way. Elijah was not as isolated as he thought. The Lord had preserved a faithful remnant: seven thousand Israelites who had never bowed their knees to Baal.

Elijah was shown that Ahab and Jezebel had not

preempted God's rule of the world; Elijah did not need to despair of God's purposes. Still more was implied in God's whispered word on Horeb. God had not forgotten His promise to Abraham and to David. Judgment must come upon Israel, but God would yet show mercy through judgment. True, Israel quickly forgot the fire that fell on Carmel, but God had another purpose beyond the showing of His power. His word would yet be spoken, a word that expressed the mystery of His salvation.

Elijah stood at the head of the long succession of prophets who ministered that word of God. Not in the thunder of Sinai, not in the fire of Carmel, but in the quiet word of revelation to His prophets, the Lord would reveal the incredible design of His saving mercy. Much later, the last of the great prophets, John the Baptist, would come in the spirit and power of Elijah to herald the fulfillment of God's design: the Lord Himself had come to save His people.

Like Elijah, John had expected fire from heaven. He thought that Jesus, the coming One, needed to cut down the wicked like trees in order to usher in the blessing of the Kingdom. When Jesus worked miracles of blessing rather than judgment, John became confused. His own denunciations of wickedness had locked him in King Herod's prison. There he heard that Jesus was even raising the dead (Lk. 7:18). But where was His work of liberation? How could the poor and the oppressed receive the blessing of God if their oppressors were not judged?

John sent his disciples to Jesus with a question: "Are you the one who was to come, or should we expect someone else?" (Lk. 7:19). Like Elijah, John looked to the Lord to bring destruction upon the enemies of God's Kingdom. Before John's disciples, Jesus performed more of His miracles, miracles that exactly fulfilled the prophecies (Is. 35:5-6). Then He said, "Blessed is the man who does not fall away on account of me" (Lk. 7:23). The quiet voice of the Lord instructed John as it had instructed Elijah. He would do His work in His way.

If the fire of holiness were indeed to descend, all must be consumed. It would be the day of judgment not only for King Herod, who had imprisoned John, but for John himself and his disciples. Jesus had come, not to bring the judgment, but to bear it. When Elijah stood with Moses on the Mount of Transfiguration, he spoke with Jesus about His coming death. It was clear that the mystery of God's redemption could be realized only through the sacrifice of Calvary.

From Elijah to John the Baptist, all the prophets were preparing for the One who was to come. Moses himself foretold the coming of a great Prophet whom the people must heed (Dt. 18:18). Prophets wrote the history of Israel, describing the faithfulness or unfaithfulness of Israel's judges and kings. They wrote a painful message of apostasy, judgment, and doom. Yet they were no mere doomsayers, looking back to memories of the past. Rather, they stood like watchmen on the walls of Jerusalem, looking for the coming salvation of the Lord (Is. 62:6-7).

When Israel entered the land under Joshua, they recited the blessings and the judgments of God's covenant, recorded in Deuteronomy 27-29. God's promises had been kept. In spite of the weary history of Israel's disobedience, God had given them the land, and Solomon could praise God for doing what He had promised. But Israel's apostasy, evident even in the reign of Solomon, brought down the judgments of Deuteronomy. Yet, in Deuteronomy 30, we see that God had promised even more. After judgment had driven Israel into exile, God would gather His people again and circumcise their hearts (Dt. 30:6).

The prophets were faithful to this message. They warned the people of the way God would use the Gentile nations as His instruments in judging Israel. They also warned the nations. The invaders who devastated Israel were not waging God's holy war. They were not the Lord's avenging holy ones as Israel was called to be as they entered Canaan. Rather, they were like rapacious beasts devouring their prey. They worshiped the dragnet of their own military might. God would indeed use them, but He would also judge them (Is. 10:5-19; 34:2-4).

Even in the midst of God's judgments on Israel, His purposes were certain to be accomplished. God had called Abraham to be a blessing to the nations. If Israel failed in that calling by disobedience, then the punishment of their disobedience would accomplish God's design. The famine that Elijah brought down on Israel brought the word of the Lord to a Gentile widow (1 Ki. 17:8-24; Lk. 4:26). Naaman, a Syrian general raised up as a scourge against Israel, was healed of his leprosy by the prophet Elisha—healed, to be sure, to continue his military career against Israel.

The fullest picture of how judgment on Israel could bring blessing to the Gentiles is found in the story of Jonah. The Lord commanded the prophet Jonah to go and preach God's sentence of judgment against Nineveh (Jon. 1:2). Jonah disobeyed the Lord; he headed in the opposite direction, taking passage on a ship headed for Tarshish in the west. His reason is clear: Nineveh was at that time the capital of the Assyrian superpower. But its armies threatened the existence of Israel. (Our only surviving representation of a king of Israel is on the "Black Obelisk" of Shalmanezer III in the British Museum.[2] The Assyrian stele shows Jehu, the king of Israel, kissing the ground before the king of Nineveh. Behind Jehu are porters carrying and leading the tribute that he brought to Assyria.)

Jonah had prophesied relief for Israel. The nation, indeed, enjoyed prosperity under Jeroboam II (2 Ki. 14:25).

But now, as he confesses at the end of the book (Jon. 4:2), Jonah is filled with dread. Suppose his prophetic warning is heeded? What if Nineveh repents of its wickedness? Will not God spare it? If Nineveh is spared, how can Israel be safe?

Jonah decided that he was expendable. God had called him to warn Nineveh that in forty days it would be destroyed. Suppose he removed himself from action: the Ninevites would not receive the warning, and Nineveh's destruction would be certain. Jonah was willing to perish so that Israel might be preserved.

His decision explains not only his scheme to take a voyage, but also the remarkable calm that enabled him to sleep through the gale that soon swept over the ship. When his identity was disclosed to the terrified sailors, he offered a second plan that seemed even more effective. Let them throw him overboard. The storm came from the Lord; Jonah was the object of God's wrath. Jonah would drown, the sailors would survive—and Nineveh would hear no warning.

Inside the great creature that God sent to rescue Jonah, the prophet confessed that salvation was of the Lord. He had gone down, as it were, to the very depths of the grave, but the Lord had spared him. Cast forth on the shore, Jonah went at last to Nineveh. He preached as God had commanded, and his worst fears were realized. The Ninevites did, indeed, repent, from the king to the lowest servant.

We see Jonah sitting outside the city, waiting for day forty, hoping against hope that Nineveh's repentance would not measure up to God's standards. He pours forth his "I told you so" to God: "O LORD, is this not what I said when I was still at home? That is why I was so quick to flee to Tarshish. I knew that you are a gracious and compassionate God, slow to anger and abounding in love, a God who relents from sending calamity. Now, O LORD, take away my life, for it is better for me to die than to live" (Jon. 4:2-3).

Jonah was right, of course, on all counts. He had reason to know God's compassion and love! He was right about Nineveh, too. Although God spared it, after some years passed armies did march from Nineveh to conquer Israel and deport its people into exile. What Jonah forgot was the calling of Israel to bear witness to God's justice and mercy so that the Gentiles might hear.

God had blessed Abraham, but also called him to be a blessing to all the families of the earth. In spite of Jonah's zeal for Israel, that sinful nation could not escape God's judgment. God spared Nineveh to use as His weapon against Israel. If Israel's sin caused God's name to be blasphemed among the nations, then in judging Israel God would make His name known. In judging Israel, God brought blessing to the nations.

Jonah's own history became a parable of hope for the exiled people of God. Swallowed up in the sea of the nations, they were not forgotten by the Lord. Salvation is of the Lord, who would indeed deliver His people, and do so by a resurrection from the dead. The sign of Jonah has its fulfillment in Jesus Christ (Mt. 16:4). Of Him it was prophetically stated that it was better for one man to die so that the nation would not perish (Jn. 11:50-52). Jesus, the obedient Servant of the Lord, did what Jonah had been willing to do in the foolishness of his disobedience. Jesus gave His life to bring salvation to the people of God. Salvation is of the Lord!

The Lord Himself must save, for the plight of sinful humanity is too desperate for any lesser savior. Ezekiel was given a vision of the people of God in their captivity. To call them God's assembly would be grotesque. They filled the valley, but they were all dead and decayed, with the bones already dry. Ezekiel did not see even ordered skeletons as he walked the vast valley of death. The Lord's question seemed absurd: "Son of man, can these bones live?" (Ezk. 37:3).

Ezekiel did not give the obvious answer. He had some knowledge of God: "O Sovereign LORD, you alone know." And so the Lord gave His prophet his most remarkable assignment. He was to address his prophetic message to the dry bones: "Dry bones, hear the word of the LORD!"

Ezekiel gives us the description of an eerie but triumphant scene. The dry bones rattled as they assembled; tendons, flesh, and skin appeared on them. Again Ezekiel prophesied, and at his word the breath of life entered the assembly: "They came to life and stood up on their feet—a vast army."

The promise of God that accompanied the vision spoke not only of delivering Israel from their graves of captivity, but also of God putting His Spirit in them that they might live. No exiled Israelite could paint a darker picture of the condition of a captive and scattered people. The situation was beyond human remedy. Only God could give the life of His Spirit to the valley of the dead. The image of Ezekiel's valley was before the apostle Paul as he described the condition of a lost world: dead in trespasses and sins (Eph. 2:1; Col. 2:13).

The Lord *had* to come, not only because man's condition was impossible but because His promises were also impossible. Abraham had laughed at the impossible promise that a son would be born of Sarah in her old age. He would have God scale down His promises and settle for Ishmael, the son of Hagar, Sarah's slave. But no word is too much for God (Gen. 18:14). Isaac, "Laughter," was born according to God's timing.

Apart from the coming of the Lord, the promises of His prophets would have been pure fantasy. They trumpeted disaster and doom, but they also announced that the Lord was not finished with His people. Isaiah pictured the felling of the cedar of Israel's pride. Was all hope, then, gone? No, because the stump of the tree remained in the ground, and a shoot would spring up to become a standard, an ensign to which the nations would be gathered (Is. 10:33-34; 11:1,10).

Two answers were given to the questions of despair that even the prophets shared. First, the destruction would not be total: God would spare a *remnant.* Second, the destruction would not be final: God would bring *renewal.* The stump of the cedar was the remaining remnant; the shoot was God's renewal.

The remnant, indeed, may have been pitifully small: like the gleanings left in the corner of a field, or a few olives missed at the top of a tree (Is. 17:6). Amos compared the remnant to a single coal left glowing from a campfire, or to the legs and ears left from a lion's kill (Amos 4:11-12). But God would keep His own. The good grain would not fall to the ground (Amos 9:9).

After the thunderstorm of judgment would come the bright rainbow of promise. God would not only deliver His people; He would take away their hearts of stone and give them hearts of flesh (Ezk. 36:26-27). He would establish a New Covenant with them (Jer. 31:31-34). Universal peace and justice would be established in a new heavens and earth (Is. 11:6-9; 65:17-25).

Indeed, streams of waters will flow down every hillside, the moon will be as bright as the sun, the Lord will heal the wounds of His people (Is. 30:23-26). A remnant from the enemy nations will be delivered along with the remnant of Israel (Jer. 48:47; 49:6; Ps. 87:4-5). And the Lord will spread His feast for all people:

> On this mountain the LORD Almighty will prepare
>   a feast of rich food for all peoples,
> a banquet of aged wine—
>   the best of meats and the finest of wines.

On this mountain he will destroy
    the shroud that enfolds all peoples,
the sheet that covers all nations;
    he will swallow up death forever.   (Is. 25:6-8)

Indeed, so inconceivable will be the overflow of blessing that both Egypt and Assyria will worship the God of Israel. The Egyptians will travel from the south right through the land of Israel to worship God in Assyria, and the Assyrians will duplicate the pilgrimage in reverse, passing Jerusalem to worship God in Egypt (Is. 19:23). The fond names given by the Lord to His covenant people will be given in blessing to these enemy nations: "Blessed be Egypt my people, Assyria my handiwork, and Israel my inheritance" (Is. 19:25).

After the return from exile, some wept at the apparent insignificance of their Temple, remembering the grandeur that was past. Where was the glory God had promised? The prophet Zechariah did not suggest that God may have promised too much, and that the people needed to be content with what they had. To the contrary, he began again to describe the indescribable: a Jerusalem where every pot is as holy as a Temple vessel, where horses' bridles carry the inscription from the gold plate of the high priest's tiara ("Holiness to the LORD"), and where the feeblest inhabitant is like King David (Zech. 12:8; 14:20-21). One question remains. In that day what will the King be like? "The house of David will be like God, like the Angel of the Lord going before them" (Zech. 12:8).

To be sure, the oracles of the prophets are full of imagery and poetry. Isaiah did not need a modern scientist to suggest to him the possible difficulty of a sun seven times brighter than that which scorched the summer fields of Israel. But the figurative language of the prophets is used to describe a blessing not less than their words, but more. In the same way, the visions given to John in the book of Revelation describe the unimaginable glory of the true and final City of God.

The Lord Will Come

The promises of the prophets soar beyond what can be expressed. They must, for it is God Himself who will fulfill them. The One who brings light brighter than the sun is the God of Glory:

> "Arise, shine, for your light has come,
>   and the glory of the LORD rises upon you.
> See, darkness covers the earth
>   and thick darkness is over the peoples,
> but the LORD rises upon you
>   and his glory appears over you." (Is. 60:1-2)

If the scattered people of God are to be gathered into one, God Himself must be their Shepherd. Ezekiel brings the word of the Lord against the false shepherds who so miserably cared for God's flock:

> "This is what the Sovereign LORD says: I am against the shepherds and will hold them accountable for my flock. I will remove them from tending the flock so that the shepherds can no longer feed themselves. . . .
>   "I myself will search for my sheep and look after them. As a shepherd looks after his scattered flock when he is with them, so will I look after my sheep." (Ezk. 34:10-12)

Isaiah powerfully and tenderly describes the Lord as the Shepherd, leading Israel back out of captivity in a second exodus deliverance. Handel, in his *Messiah*, has set that

Scripture to music: "He shall feed his flock like a shepherd: he shall gather the lambs with his arm, and carry them in his bosom, and shall gently lead those that are with young" (Is. 40:11, KJV).

The Lord will come as a Warrior as well as a Shepherd. In a world of exploitation and injustice, where truth is nowhere to be found, the Lord looks and is displeased:

> He saw that there was no one,
>> he was appalled that there was no one to
>>> intervene;
> so his own arm worked salvation for him,
>> and his own righteousness sustained him.
> He put on righteousness as his breastplate,
>> and the helmet of salvation on his head;
> he put on the garments of vengeance
>> and wrapped himself in zeal as in a cloak.
>>>> (Is. 59:16-17)

The shepherds and judges of God's people have all failed; they need a divine Savior. Salvation means deliverance from the evil oppressors who prey on the people of God. God will come in power to destroy those who hold them captive. Yet their captivity is darker, their dungeon deeper than anything arms can enforce. They are held captives by their own sins. Micah therefore proclaims that God will triumph, not only over their enemies, but over their sins. When God shows His salvation, nations will see, be ashamed, and fear:

> Who is a God like you,
>> who pardons sin and forgives the transgression
>> of the remnant of his inheritance?
> You do not stay angry forever

but delight to show mercy.
You will again have compassion on us;
    you will tread our sins underfoot
    and hurl all our iniquities into the depths of
        the sea.   (Mic. 7:18-19)

God has the power to save. No foe can resist the divine Warrior whose chariots are the clouds. The miracles of the exodus, the fall of Jericho, the victories of David, all showed God's power. But the prophets proclaim an even deeper salvation. The Lord must not only free His people from chains; He must free them from sin. To free His people, God must capture their hearts.

God comes, therefore, not just in the majesty of His power, but in the compassion of His love. The Warrior and Judge who is also a Shepherd cares for His people: "He said, 'Surely they are my people, sons who will not be false to me'; and so he became their Savior. In all their distress he too was distressed, and the angel of his presence saved them. In love and mercy he redeemed them; he lifted them up and carried them all the days of old" (Is. 63:8-9).

Indeed, the Shepherd of Israel is Husband and Father to His people. The prophet Hosea is directed to take back Gomer, his adulterous wife, to show the love of God for apostate Israel. The figures are combined in Ezekiel, where the Lord is described as finding Israel as an abandoned baby girl cast out in the open field, still in the blood of her birth. The Lord grants her life, growth to maturity, cleanses and clothes her, and makes her His bride (Ezk. 16:1-14), only to have her turn from Him to other lovers and use His gifts to seduce them.

Israel's lovers turned against her and became God's instruments in judging her. Yet at the last, God would reestablish His covenant. His people would eventually repent, and be ashamed: "So I will establish my covenant with you, and you will know that I am the LORD. Then, when I make atonement for you for all you have done, you will remember and be ashamed and never again open your mouth because of your humiliation, declares the Sovereign LORD" (Ezk. 16:62-63).

The figure changes: as Father, God leads His little son, Israel, out of Egypt, holding him by the hand and teaching him to walk (Hos. 11:3). His son's rebellion brings judgment, but the Lord cries out:

> "How can I give you up, Ephraim?
>> How can I hand you over, Israel?
> How can I treat you like Admah?
>> How can I make you like Zeboiim?
> My heart is changed within me;
>> all my compassion is aroused.
> I will not carry out my fierce anger,
>> nor will I turn and devastate Ephraim.
> For I am God, and not man—
>> the Holy One among you.
> I will not come in wrath."   (Hos. 11:8-9)

The prophet's oracle goes on to declare that the Lord will roar like a lion to gather His children from the west and the east.

When the Lord comes to judge and to save, the very trees of the wood will sing for joy before Him (Ps. 96:12-13), and His people will join the song:

> "Sing, O Daughter of Zion;
>> shout aloud, O Israel!
> Be glad and rejoice with all your heart,
>> O Daughter of Jerusalem!

The LORD has taken away your punishment,
    he has turned back your enemy.
The LORD, the King of Israel, is with you;
    never again will you fear any harm. . . .
The LORD your God is with you,
    he is mighty to save.
He will take great delight in you,
    he will quiet you with his love,
    he will rejoice over you with singing."
                        (Zeph. 3:14-15,17)

The Servant of the Lord Will Come

God's word of promise will not return empty. His grace will not be frustrated. His compassion will triumph. The dreadful destruction of His wrath against apostasy will not be total or final, for God purposes salvation beyond imagining.

Yet God is not mocked. There must be a response to His love. If He is Lord, then He must be loved and served as Lord. If He is Father, He must claim His true son. Unless our disobedience is overcome, God's coming must be feared rather than welcomed: "Who can endure the day of his coming? Who can stand when he appears?" (Mal. 3:2).

God had kept His covenant; His people were the covenant-breakers. If there was to be a new covenant of promise, it was not enough for God to come in glory. The people, too, had to be represented. Abraham, Isaac, Jacob, Joseph, Moses, Joshua, Samson, Samuel, David, Solomon, Elijah, Elisha, Jonah, Isaiah, Jeremiah, Daniel—all the prophets, priests, and kings of Israel fell far short. They led Israel, prayed for the people, reasoned with the people, fought for them and contended with them, but they could not keep God's covenant for them. They could not stand in the place of the people, or take their part. A greater Savior was needed.

That Savior, too, would come. Keeping pace with the

promise that the Lord would come is the promise that the
Servant would come: a Prophet like Moses, but a better
Mediator; a Priest like Aaron, but One of the royal order of
Melchizedek; a King like David, but given an eternal throne.
The new humanity needed to be founded by a second Adam,
the descendant of the woman who would crush the serpent's
head. The promise to Abraham was to be fulfilled in another
Isaac, the true Seed in whom the nations would be blessed.
The new Israel had to be established in the Person of the
Lord's Servant. Here is the declaration of that individual
Servant:

> He said to me, "You are my servant,
>> Israel, in whom I will display my splendor." . . .
> And now the LORD says—
>> he who formed me in the womb to be his servant
> to bring Jacob back to him
>> and gather Israel to himself. . . .
> "It is too small a thing for you to be my servant
>> to restore the tribes of Jacob
> and bring back those of Israel I have kept.
> I will also make you a light for the Gentiles,
>> that you may bring my salvation to the ends of
>> the earth."   (Is. 49:3-6)

God's Servant was to be identified with Israel, and
called by the name of Israel, yet He would also be distinguished from Israel, for He would bring back and restore
those who would be preserved of Israel, and be God's light to
the Gentiles. God's calling and choosing of Israel had been
mocked as Israel chose other gods. God would therefore
choose His Servant, and put His Spirit upon Him (Is. 42:1).
God's Servant would fulfill the calling of Israel among the
nations, and in Him the new and true Israel would be estab-

lished (Ro. 9:6-8; 15:8-9).

God's elect Servant was to be His delight, yet He would be called to humiliation and suffering. The enemies of the Lord would be His enemies; the reproaches directed to God would be heaped upon Him (Ps. 69:9). The astonishing message regarding God's Suffering Servant brought to a climax the ministry of the prophets (Is. 53).

The sufferings of God's Servant would be brutal and astonishing. Men would stand aghast at the abuse He suffered. He was to be a man of agony—beaten, bruised, scourged, wounded, and executed. He was to be disfigured in His afflictions until His appearance was scarcely human. He would be without beauty; no one would want Him. He would experience grief, abandonment, dereliction: a man of sorrows, and acquainted with grief. The proud and powerful would despise Him as insignificant; people would accuse Him as reprobate. Do not His tortures mark Him as one rejected by God?

Yet the Servant was to endure all this with submissive meekness. He would be righteous and innocent, yet He would not resist. He was to be led as a lamb to the slaughter, or as a sheep to be sheared.

More amazing still, there would be meaning in His tragedy. The agonizing death of God's Servant was to be a sacrifice. He would suffer by God's decree (Is. 53:10). He was not a transgressor, yet He was to be numbered with the transgressors, for He would bear the sins of the many. We were like sheep who had gone astray, but the Lord would lay on Him the iniquity of us all. "After arrest and sentence he was taken away, and who cared where he went? He was cut off out of the land of the living, stricken with death for the transgression of my people" (Is. 53:8).[3] His soul was to be made an offering for sin (v. 10).

He would suffer as the substitute for those to whom the

stroke was due. He would do so willingly, for He would actively bear their griefs, sorrows, and sicknesses. He would make intercession for the transgressors. By His welts they would be healed.

The sacrifice of the Servant would issue in victory, a royal and priestly victory proclaimed to the nations. He was to be a royal Victor. God's triumphant Servant was to be a complete success, exalted and lifted up on high (52:13). The Lord's pleasure would prosper in His hand. He would justify many, and would share with them the spoils of His triumph. As a Priest, He would sprinkle many nations, and would intercede for sinners. The nations would hear with astonishment the meaning of His sufferings.

Here at last is the culmination of the long story of the suffering of the servants of God. Moses endured the reproach of Israel. Elijah fled for his life. Jeremiah was cast into a pit. But Isaiah describes One who is more than a prophet. Like them, He is persecuted, but unlike them, He is sinless. David, too, bore reproach for the sake of the Lord, but David brought shame on his rule by his own sin. The Lord delivered him and restored his throne, but David was never exalted to God's right hand. The priests offered daily sacrifices, but the Servant offers Himself as the sin offering. The anointing of the Servant is with the Holy Spirit; the ministry of the Servant is to accomplish God's salvation to the ends of the earth.

In the message of the prophets, the coming of God's anointed Servant is drawn ever more closely to the coming of God Himself. When God comes to be the Shepherd of His people, David will be their shepherd (Ezk. 34:23). When the least citizen of Jerusalem will be like King David, the House of David will be as God, as the Angel of the Lord before them (Zech. 12:8). The divine names are given to the promised King: "For to us a child is born, to us a son is given, and the government will be on his shoulders. And he will be called Wonderful Counselor, Mighty God, Everlasting Father, Prince of Peace" (Is. 9:6).

The name "Mighty God" is attributed to the Lord by Isaiah in the next chapter (Is. 10:21). How, then, can it be borne by the Messiah? "Therefore the Lord himself will give you a sign: The virgin will be with child and will give birth to a son, and will call him Immanuel" ("God with us"—Is. 7:14).

Since Adam was made in the image of God, there is a sense in which he can be called God's son (Lk. 3:38). Angels, too, are called sons of God in the Old Testament (Job 1:6). But in the exaltation of the royal Messiah, a unique Sonship is ascribed to Him (Ps. 2:6; cf. Ps. 72). Jesus reminded His critics that David addressed his promised Son as his Lord (Ps. 110:1; Mt. 22:43-45). The Angel of the covenant who would come to His Temple was none other than the Lord Himself (Mal. 3:1). Malachi, the last of the Old Testament prophets, predicted the coming of Elijah as His herald (Mal. 4:5). John the Baptist, coming in the Spirit and power of Elijah, fulfilled that promise, and proclaimed the coming of the One whose shoes he was not worthy to untie. His was a voice crying in the wilderness, "Prepare the way of the Lord!"

The story of Jesus in the Old Testament becomes the gospel story in the New. In the miracle of the Incarnation, the Lord Himself comes to provide the salvation of His people. "No word is impossible for God"—His promise to Sarah was kept to Mary (Gen. 18:14; Lk. 1:37). The virgin conceived as the angel had promised: "The Holy Spirit will come upon you, and the power of the Most High will overshadow you. So the holy one to be born will be called the Son of God" (Lk. 1:35). He who was born of Mary was not only the Lord's Christ (Lk. 2:26); He was, as the angel said, Christ the

Lord (Lk. 2:11). He came as a light to the Gentiles and the glory of Israel (Lk. 2:32). "And the Word became flesh, and tabernacled among us (and we beheld his glory, glory as of the only begotten from the Father), full of grace and truth" (Jn. 1:14, ASV margin). "No one has ever seen God, but God the Only Begotten, who is at the Father's side, has made him known" (Jn. 1:18, NIV margin). Jesus could say, "'I and the Father are one.' . . . Anyone who has seen me has seen the Father" (Jn. 10:30; 14:9).

As Lord, Jesus commanded the storms and the demons. He walked on the waves and raised the dead at the word of His command. He spoke with authority, forgiving sins and claiming the worship of His disciples. Thomas fell at His feet when he saw the risen Lord, confessing, "My Lord and my God!" Peter acknowledged for them all that Jesus was the Christ, the Son of the living God (Mt. 16:16).

Years after Christ's ascension, Peter wrote to the Christians in Asia Minor, encouraging them as they faced persecution for Christ's sake. He quoted from the prophecy of Isaiah, where Isaiah says, "Fear not their fear, nor be frightened . . ." (Is. 8:12, Septuagint). But where Isaiah continues, "Sanctify the Lord himself," Peter writes instead, "Sanctify the Lord, the Christ" (1 Pet. 3:15, literal translation). For Peter, Christ Jesus, who had slept in his fishing boat, was to be hallowed as the Lord Himself.

Christ the Lord is confessed as God the Son in the New Testament. He is also revealed as the Servant. He comes to do the will of His Father, to give His life as a ransom for many. Israel was God's vine in the prophets (Is. 5), but Jesus Christ is the true Vine. He fulfills the ministry of the circumcision for the truth of God, that He may confirm the promises given to the fathers, and that the Gentiles might glorify God for His mercy (Ro. 15:8-9).

Though He was tempted in all points as we are, He was

without sin. He fulfilled all righteousness. Resolutely He went to His death on the cross: "He himself bore our sins in his body on the tree, so that we might die to sins and live for righteousness; by his wounds you have been healed" (1 Pet. 2:24).

On the third day He rose from the dead, showed Himself to His disciples for forty days, then ascended into heaven to receive His glory at the Father's right hand. He sealed His victory over sin and death by sending the Spirit from the throne. Now He is Lord of the universe, and Head of His body, the church. All of history unfolds to complete the story of Jesus, until the day that He comes again.

> He is the image of the invisible God, the firstborn over all creation. For by him all things were created: things in heaven and on earth, visible and invisible, whether thrones or powers or rulers or authorities; all things were created by him and for him. He is before all things, and in him all things hold together. And he is the head of the body, the church; he is the beginning and the firstborn from among the dead, so that in everything he might have the supremacy. For God was pleased to have all his fullness dwell in him, and through him to reconcile to himself all things, whether things on earth or things in heaven, by making peace through his blood, shed on the cross. (Col. 1:15-20)

NOTES:
1. "Busy" in the NIV translation is a euphemism. Elijah's taunt was more earthy. The business he suggested had to do with the toilet.
2. J.D. Douglas, *The Illustrated Bible Dictionary*, Part 2, page 742.
3. For this translation, see Henri Blocher, *Songs of the Servant* (Downers Grove, Ill.: InterVarsity Press, 1975), page 64.

INDEX OF SCRIPTURE

206 / Index of Scripture

105:16-19—81
109:21—156
110—137-38, 159, 165
110:1—14, 153, 158, 163, 200
118:14—96
118:26—163
132—165
147:18-19—170

Proverbs
3:5—170
3:7—170
3:19—170
8—174
8:22—170
8:22-31—170
9:10—170
12:15—170
23:10-11—155
30:4—68, 120

Ecclesiastes
1:2—171
2:16—171
5:15—171
8:17—172
11:5—172
12:13-14—172

Isaiah
5—201
7:14—200
8:12—201
8:17f.—39
9:5-6—165
9:6—199-200
10:5-19—186
10:21—200
10:33-34—190

11:1—190
11:6-9—190
11:10—190
12:2—96
17:6—190
19:23—191
19:25—191
25:6-8—190-91
25:8—172
30:23-26—190
30:30-32—124
34:2-4—186
35:4-6—118
35:5-6—184
40:11—193
42:1—197
43:1—156
43:7—93
43:14—156
43:15—163
44:22-23—156
48:20—156
49:3—76
49:3-6—197
52:3—156
52:13—199
53—198
53:4—118
53:5—118
53:6—120
53:8—198
53:10—198
59:16-17—15, 193
60:1-2—192
61:1-2—118
62:6-7—185
63:8-9—194
63:9—124, 156
63:16—156
65:17-25—190

Jeremiah
23:5-6—165
25:4—180
30:9—165
30:17—118
31:3—154
31:31-34—190
33:6—118
34:18-20—47
48:47—190
49:6—190
50:34—156

Ezekiel
16:1-14—194
16:62-63—195
34:1-10—151
34:10-12—192
34:23—199
34:23-24—165
36:26-27—190
37:3—188
37:21-25—165
47:12—118

Daniel
7:13-14—119

Hosea
11:3—195
11:8-9—195
12:2-6—73

Amos
4:11-12—190
9:9—190
9:11—165

Jonah
1:2—186
2:9—12